Dr.Jekyll and Mr.Hyde

# 지킬 박사와 하이드 씨

# 지킬 박사와 하이드 씨



First edition: October 2011

TEL (02)2000-0515 | FAX (02)2271-0172
ISBN 978-89-17-23788-7

# YBM Reading Library 는...

쉬운 영어로 문학 작품을 즐기면서 영어 실력을 크게 향상시킬 수 있도록 개발된 독해력 완성 프로젝트입니다. 전 세계 어린이와 청소년들에게 재미와 감동을 주는 세계의 명작을 이제 영어로 읽으세요. 원작에 보다 가까이 다가가는 재미와 명작의 깊이를 느낄 수 있을 거예요.

350 단어에서 1800 단어까지 6단계로 나누어져 있어 초·중·고 어느 수준에서나 자신이 좋아하는 스토리를 골라 읽을 수 있고, 눈에 쉽게 들어오는 기본 문장을 바탕으로 활용도가 높고 세련된 영어 표현을 구사하기 때문에 쉽게 읽으면서 영어의 맛을 느낄 수 있습니다. 상세한 해설과 흥미로운 학습 정보, 퀴즈 등이 곳곳에 숨어 있어 학습 효과를 더욱 높일 수 있습니다.

이야기의 분위기를 멋지게 재현해 주는 삽화를 보면서 재미있는 이야기를 읽고, 전문 성우들의 박진감 있는 연기로 스토리를 반복해서 듣다 보면 리스닝 실력까지 크게 향상됩니다.

세계의 명작을 읽는 재미와 영어 실력 완성의 기쁨을 마음껏 맛보고 싶다면, YBM Reading Library와 함께 지금 출발하세요!

# YBM Reading Library

책을 읽기 전에 가볍게 워밍업을 한 다음, 재미있게 스토리를 읽고, 다 읽고 난 후 주요 구문과 리스닝까지 꼭꼭 다지는 3단계 리딩 전략! YBM Reading Library, 이렇게 활용 하세요.

## Before the Story

### People in the Story
스토리에 들어가기 전, 등장인물과 만나며 이야기의 분위기를 느껴 보세요~

## In the Story

### ★ 스토리
재미있는 스토리를 읽어요. 잘 모른다고 멈추지 마세요. 한 페이지, 또는 한 chapter를 끝까지 읽으면서 흐름을 파악하세요.

### ★★ 단어 및 구문 설명
어려운 단어나 문장을 마주쳤을 때, 그 뜻이 알고 싶다면 여기를 보세요. 나중에 꼭 외우는 것은 기본이죠.

---

"That's a good observation," said Mr. Utterson. "But there is one question. Do you know the name of the man who walked over the child?"

"His name was Hyde," said Mr. Enfield.

"Hmmm," said Mr. Utterson. "What does he look like?"

"Well, it is not easy to describe his appearance," said Mr. Enfield. "He's a strange-looking man. He is short, but has a strong, heavy body. There's something ugly and unpleasant about him. I disliked him at once."

★ "Interesting," said Mr. Utterson. "Well, Richard, I know who the man who signed the check is because I've actually heard something of this story before. Are you certain about everything you've told me?"

"Yes," said Mr. Enfield. "I've described everything exactly as it occurred. Hyde had a key and he still has it because I saw him use it again a few days ago."

Mr. Utterson sighed deeply but said nothing.

★★
- ☐ observation 관찰
- ☐ describe 묘사하다, 설명하다
- ☐ appearance 외모, 특징
- ☐ unpleasant 불쾌한, 기분 나쁜
- ☐ dislike 싫어하다, 혐오하다
- ☐ at once 보자마자, 즉시
- ☐ be certain about …에 대해 확신하다
- ☐ occur 일어나다, 발생하다 (occur - occurred - occurred)
- ☐ sigh deeply 깊은 한숨을 쉬다

### ★★★ 돌발 퀴즈
스토리를 잘 파악하고 있는지 궁금하면 돌발 퀴즈로 잠깐 확인해 보세요.

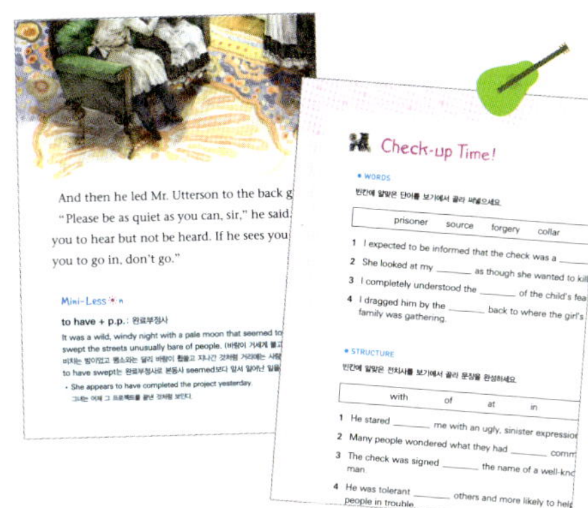

**Mini-Lesson**
너무나 중요해서 그냥 지나칠 수 없는
알짜 구문은 별도로 깊이 있게 배워요.

**Check-up Time!**
한 chapter를 다 읽은 후 어휘, 구문,
summary까지 확실하게 다져요.

**Focus on Background**
작품 뒤에 숨겨져 있는 흥미로운 이야기를
읽으세요. 상식까지 풍부해집니다.

## After the Story

**Reading X-File**  이야기 속에 등장했던
주요 구문을 재미있는 설명과 함께 다시 한번~

**Listening X-File**  영어 발음과 리스닝 실력을 함께
다져 주는 중요한 발음법칙을 살펴봐요.

## MP3 Files
www.ybmbooksam.com에서 다운로드 하세요!

# Dr. Jekyll and Mr. Hyde

# Robert Louis Stevenson
## (1850 ~ 1894)

로버트 루이스 스티븐슨은 …

스코틀랜드 에딘버러(Edinburgh)에서 태어났다. 부유한 토목기사인 아버지의 뒤를 잇기 위해 에딘버러 공대에 진학했지만, 적성에 맞지 않아 법학과로 전과하여 변호사가 되었다. 그 후 그는 폐결핵으로 건강이 악화되자 요양을 위해 세계 각지를 여행하며 지역적 특색이 묻어나는 작품들을 쓰기 시작했다.

잡지에 여행기와 단편소설을 기고하던 스티븐슨은 대표작인 〈보물섬(Treasure Island, 1883)〉으로 단숨에 인기 작가로의 명성을 얻게 된다. 그 후 〈납치(Kidnapped, 1886)〉, 〈지킬 박사와 하이드 씨(Dr. Jekyll and Mr. Hyde, 1886)〉, 〈발란트레 경(The Master of Ballantrae, 1889)〉, 〈카트리오나(Catriona, 1893)〉 등과 같은 화제작을 잇따라 발표하며 세계적인 작가로의 입지를 굳혔다.

평생 병마에 시달리면서도 모험과 환상이라는 주제를 기반으로 탁월한 상상력을 발휘하며 열정적으로 창작 활동에 몰두했던 스티븐슨은 영문학사에서 환상 문학의 한 획을 그은 작가로 평가 받고 있다.

# Dr. Jekyll and Mr. Hyde

지킬 박사와 하이드 씨는 …

로버트 루이스 스티븐슨의 대표작 중 하나로 한 인간의 내부에서 계속되는 선과 악의 대결, 그리고 인간의 이중적인 도덕성으로 인해 끊임없이 대립하는 자아의 내면을 미스터리 형식으로 풀어낸 작품이다.

유복한 집안에서 태어나 의사로서 만인의 존경을 받는 지킬 박사는 겉으로는 완벽한 삶을 살아간다. 하지만 금지된 쾌락의 유혹을 억제하지 못해 괴로워하던 그는 선과 악을 분리하는 약을 개발하기 위한 실험을 시작한다. 드디어 약 개발에 성공하여 약을 복용하자 악한 본성인 하이드가 깨어나 마음껏 악행을 저지르고 일탈을 만끽한다. 하지만 그의 선한 본성마저 하이드의 지배를 받게 되자 선한 본성인 지킬이 영원히 사라지기 직전 스스로 목숨을 끊음으로써 생을 마감한다.

〈지킬 박사와 하이드 씨〉는 선과 악의 대립 속에서 한 인간이 겪는 갈등을 세밀한 심리 묘사와 극적인 구조로 그려낸 수작으로 오늘날까지도 영화, 뮤지컬, 연극 등 다양한 장르로 끊임없이 재창조되어 전 세계인의 사랑을 받고 있다.

# People in the Story

〈지킬 박사와 하이드 씨〉에 등장하는 인물들을 살펴볼까요?

## Mr. Utterson

지킬 박사의 오랜 친구 변호사. 지킬 박사가 하이드의 협박을 받는 것으로 생각하고 그를 구하기 위해 풀과 함께 동분서주한다.

## Poole

지킬 박사 저택의 집사. 지킬 박사가 이상한 행동을 보일 때마다 어터슨과 상의하여 문제를 해결하기 위해 노력한다.

## Dr. Lanyon

지킬 박사의 친구이자 동료 의사. 지킬 박사가 하이드로 변하는 모습을 보고 충격을 받아 몇 주 후 세상을 뜬다.

Dr. Jekyll
런던의 명망 높은 의사. 인간
선악의 이중성을 분류하는 실험
끝에 약을 개발하여 복용하지만
점차 악의 지배를 받게 된다.

Mr. Hyde
지킬 박사의 악성을 지닌
인물. 런던을 공포에
몰아넣는 살인을 저지르고
경찰에 쫓기는 신세가 된다.

# Dr. Jekyll and Mr. Hyde

Robert Louis Stevenson

# CHAPTER 1

# The Story of the Door

문 이야기

The lawyer, Mr. G. J. Utterson, was a tall, thin man. He was strict with himself and he never showed his [1] feelings but he was somewhat lovable. He was tolerant of others and more likely to help people in trouble than disapprove them.

Every Sunday, he went for a long walk with his closest friend, Richard Enfield. Mr. Enfield was a distant cousin of Mr. Utterson and well-known man about town. Because their characters were so different, many people wondered what they had in common. The truth was that they felt comfortable in each other's company.

On one of their Sunday walks, the two men walked down a small street in a busy part of London.

---

1 **be strict with** …에게 엄격하다
He was strict with himself and he never showed his feelings.
그는 스스로에게 엄격했고 절대 자신의 감정을 드러내지 않았다.

The buildings were clean and freshly painted. Two doors down from one corner, on the opposite side of the street, was the entry to a courtyard.

□ somewhat  약간, 조금
□ be tolerant of  …에 관대하다
□ be likely to + 동사원형  …하는 경향이 있다
□ disapprove  못마땅해〔탐탁찮아〕하다
□ distant cousin  먼〔친척 관계의〕사촌
□ well-known  유명한, 잘 알려진
□ man about town  풍류가

□ have ... in common  …을 공통점으로 가지다
□ in one's company  …의 곁에서
□ freshly painted  새로 페인트가 칠해진
□ opposite  맞은편의
□ entry to  …로 들어가는 입구
□ courtyard  뜰, 마당

And just beyond that was a two-storied building which, unlike all the other houses, needed a coat of paint. It had a door on the lower floor but no windows facing the street.

When they came near the building, Mr. Enfield lifted up his cane and pointed.

"That door reminds me of an unusual story," he said.

"Indeed?" said Mr. Utterson, "and what was that?"

"I was walking home about three o'clock one morning," said Mr. Enfield, "when I noticed a little man hurrying along the street. A girl of about ten was running as hard as she could down a side street. At the [1] corner, the two collided and the girl fell heavily to the ground and she began screaming. What happened next was horrifying. The man trampled calmly over [2] her little body. I ran after him and seized him. But although he appeared perfectly calm, he stared at me with an ugly, sinister expression.*

이 부분에는 왜 "이 없을까요?
대화문이 여러 문단으로 이루어진 경우
문단의 시작마다 "을 쓰지만 "은
최종으로 끝나는 부분에 쏩니다.

□ two-storied  2층의
□ face  …로 향하다
□ lift up  …을 들어올리다
□ cane  지팡이
□ remind A of B  A에게 B를 생각나게 하다
□ collide  부딪히다, 충돌하다

□ fall to the ground  땅에 쓰러지다
□ horrifying  무시무시한
□ run after  …을 뒤쫓다
□ seize  붙잡다
□ stare at  …을 응시하다
□ sinister  사악한, 불길한
□ expression  표정

1  **as + 부사 + as + 주어 + 동사**  …가 할 수 있는 한 가장 ～하게
A girl of about ten was running as hard as she could down a side street.
열 살 정도 된 소녀가 할 수 있는 한 가장 빠르게 거리를 뛰어가고 있었어요.

2  **trample over**  …을 짓밟다
The man trampled calmly over her little body.
그 남자는 조용하게 그녀의 작은 몸을 짓밟았어요.

"I dragged him by the collar back to where the girl's family was gathering around the screaming child. Moments later, a doctor arrived and said she was not injured. Her screams came from fear, not pain. I completely understood the source of the child's fear because I had taken an instant dislike to the man. [1] The girl's family was all staring at him with expressions of hate but it was the doctor whose reaction most interested me. He didn't appear to be the emotional type but, like the rest of us, he looked at my prisoner as though he wanted to kill him.

1 take a dislike to …가 싫어지다
I had taken an instant dislike to the man.
저는 즉각 그 남자가 싫어졌어요.

"'You can't walk away,' the doctor said to him.
'If you do, we'll create a scandal that will ruin you.'

"'Naturally, I want to avoid that,' said the man.
'If you forget about this, I'll give the child some money.
Name your price.'



□ drag ... by the collar ⋯의
목덜미를 잡고 끌고 가다
□ gather around ⋯주위에 모이다
□ source 원인, 이유
□ instant 즉각적인, 순간의
□ reaction 반응
□ emotional 감정적인

□ prisoner 붙잡힌 사람
□ as though 마치 ⋯인 것처럼
□ scandal 추문, 소문
□ ruin 파멸시키다, 망치다
□ naturally 당연히, 물론
□ name 구체적으로 말하다, 지적하다

"We asked for a hundred pounds and, surprisingly, he didn't argue. He went to that door, took out a key and disappeared inside. A few minutes later he came back with ten pounds in gold and a check for ninety pounds. The check was signed with the name of a well-known man. When I said I didn't believe the signature was his, he offered to stay with us until morning and cash the check himself. So the doctor, the child's father and I took the man to my rooms, where we spent the night. Early the next day, we accompanied him to the bank where I expected to be informed that the check was a forgery. To my [1] surprise, it was genuine."

"Well," said Mr. Utterson. "That's a shocking story."

---

- □ surprisingly 놀랍게도
- □ be signed with the name of
  …의 이름으로 서명되다
- □ signature 서명
- □ offer to + 동사원형 …하는 것을 제안하다
- □ cash the check 수표를 현금으로 바꾸다
- □ accompany A to B
  B까지 A와 동행하다
- □ forgery 위조된 것
- □ genuine 진짜의, 위조가 아닌
- □ disgusting 불쾌한, 거슬리는
- □ charity work 자선 활동
- □ highly unlikely 매우 가능성이 낮은
- □ respectable 존경할 만한, 훌륭한
- □ rundown 낡은, 허물어져 가는
- □ scarcely 분명히 … 아닌

---

1  **be informed that절** …을 알게〔통보 받게〕 되다
We accompanied him to the bank where I expected to be informed that the check was a forgery.
저희는 그 수표가 위조된 것이라는 것을 알게 되리라 기대되는 은행까지 그와 동행했어요.

"Yes, it is," said Mr. Enfield. "And he's a horrible, disgusting man. But the person who signed the check is a good man and well known for his charity work."

"Do you know whether the person who signed the check lives there?"

"No, but it's highly unlikely that a respectable person would live in that rundown place, isn't it?" said Mr. Enfield.

"And you never asked him about the place with the door?" said Mr. Utterson.

"No, I didn't," said Mr. Enfield. "But I've studied it and it seems scarcely a house. There's no other entrance and nobody uses that door except, occasionally, the man. There are three windows looking onto the courtyard from the second floor. There are none on the lower floor. The windows are always closed. There's usually smoke from the chimney so I think somebody lives there."

## Mini-Less☀n

### until *vs.* by

until과 by는 '…까지'라는 뜻의 전치사인데요, until은 그 시점까지 계속되는 '진행'에 중점을 둔 표현이고, by는 그 시점까지 끝나는 '완료'에 중점을 둔 표현이랍니다.

- When I said I didn't believe the signature was his, he offered to stay with us until morning.  제가 서명이 그의 것인지 믿지 못하겠다고 말하자, 그는 아침까지 우리와 함께 있겠다고 제안했어요.
- By this time next week we may return to London.
  다음주 이맘때까지 우리는 런던에 돌아와 있을 것이다.

"That's a good observation," said Mr. Utterson. "But there is one question. Do you know the name of the man who walked over the child?"

"His name was Hyde," said Mr. Enfield.

"Hmmm," said Mr. Utterson. "What does he look like?"

"Well, it is not easy to describe his appearance," said Mr. Enfield. "He's a strange-looking man. He is short, but has a strong, heavy body. There's something ugly and unpleasant about him. I disliked him at once."

"Interesting," said Mr. Utterson. "Well, Richard, I know who the man who signed the check is because I've actually heard something of this story before. Are you certain about everything you've told me?"

"Yes," said Mr. Enfield. "I've described everything exactly as it occurred. Hyde had a key and he still has it because I saw him use it again a few days ago."

Mr. Utterson sighed deeply but said nothing.

---

□ observation 관찰
□ describe 묘사하다, 설명하다
□ appearance 외모, 특징
□ unpleasant 불쾌한, 기분 나쁜
□ dislike 싫어하다, 혐오하다

□ at once 보자마자, 즉시
□ be certain about …에 대해 확신하다
□ occur 일어나다, 발생하다
  (occur - occurred - occurred)
□ sigh deeply 깊은 한숨을 쉬다

Which is not true about Hyde?
a. He is short and has a strong body.
b. There is something ugly about him.
c. His appearance is easy to describe.

# Check-up Time!



● **WORDS**

빈칸에 알맞은 단어를 보기에서 골라 써넣으세요.

| prisoner | source | forgery | collar |
|---|---|---|---|

**1** I expected to be informed that the check was a ________.

**2** She looked at my ________ as though she wanted to kill him.

**3** I completely understood the ________ of the child's fear.

**4** I dragged him by the ________ back to where the girl's family was gathering.

● **STRUCTURE**

빈칸에 알맞은 전치사를 보기에서 골라 문장을 완성하세요.

| with | of | at | in |
|---|---|---|---|

**1** He stared ________ me with an ugly, sinister expression.

**2** Many people wondered what they had ________ common.

**3** The check was signed ________ the name of a well-known man.

**4** He was tolerant ________ others and more likely to help people in trouble.

ANSWERS

Words | 1. forgery　2. prisoner　3. source　4. collar
Structure | 1. at　2. in　3. with　4. of

## ● COMPREHENSION

본문의 내용과 일치하면 T에, 일치하지 않으면 F에 표시하세요.

T  F

**1** Hyde had a key to the two-storied house. ☐ ☐

**2** Mr. Utterson was strict with others and liked to show his feelings. ☐ ☐

**3** Mr. Enfield and Mr. Utterson had similar characters. ☐ ☐

**4** The windows of the two-storied house were always closed. ☐ ☐

## ● SUMMARY

빈칸에 맞는 말을 골라 이야기를 완성하세요.

When the lawyer, Mr. Utterson and his cousin, Mr. Enfield went for a walk, they came near a two-storied house. Mr. Enfield told Mr. Utterson an unusual story about the house and a man named Hyde. He (      ) over a little girl and his (      ) made people feel unpleasant. When Hyde was (      ), he gave the girl's family ten pounds in gold and a check for ninety pounds. Mr. Enfield was suspicious of the check, but it was proved to be (      ).

a. threatened      b. trampled

c. genuine      d. appearance

ANSWERS

Comprehension 1.T 2.F 3.F 4.T
Summary 1.b, d, a, c

# CHAPTER 2

# The Search for Mr. Hyde

하이드 씨를 찾아서

As soon as he had eaten dinner that evening, Mr. Utterson went into his office, opened his safe and took out an envelope. It contained the will of Dr. Henry Jekyll.

Mr. Utterson sat down at his desk and read the document. It stated that in case of Henry Jekyll's death, all his possessions were to pass into the hands of his dear friend, Edward Hyde. And in the unlikely case of Dr. Jekyll's "disappearance or unexplained absence" for more than three months, Edward Hyde would also inherit everything. Mr. Utterson thought the conditions of inheritance, although not unlawful, were unnatural and immoral. He had refused to help Jekyll write it.

---

- □ contain 포함하다
- □ will 유언장
- □ state that절 …을 (문서에) 명시하다
- □ in case of …의 경우에
- □ possession (주로 복수형으로) 소유물, 재산
- □ pass into the hands of …의 손에 들어가다
- □ absence 부재(不在)
- □ inherit 상속받다, 물려받다
- □ condition (요구)조건
- □ inheritance 상속
- □ unlawful 불법의
- □ immoral 비도덕적인
- □ madness 미친 짓
- □ butler 집사
- □ usher 안내하다
- □ hearty (마음이) 따뜻한, 다정한

"I believed it was madness," he thought, "but now I'm sure there is something truly evil about this. I must discuss this with my friend Dr. Lanyon tonight. If anyone knows about Mr. Hyde, he will."

He put on a heavy coat and went out and was soon knocking on the door of a large house in Cavendish Square. The butler welcomed him and ushered him directly from the door to the dining room, where Dr. Lanyon sat. He was a healthy, hearty gentleman, with thick white hair.

**be to + 동사원형**

be동사 뒤에 「to + 동사원형」이 오면 '…할 것이다' 라는 예정 혹은 '…해야 하다' 라는 의무의 뜻이 된답니다.

- All his possessions were to pass into the hands of his dear friend, Edward Hyde.
  그의 모든 재산은 그의 친애하는 친구인 에드워드 하이드의 손에 들어갈 것이다.
- She was to help her sister for her wedding.  그녀는 언니의 결혼식을 위해 언니를 도와야 했다.

After some small talk, Mr. Utterson began to speak about what was on his mind.

"I must talk to you about Henry Jekyll," he said. "We are probably his two oldest friends, aren't we?"

"I suppose so," said the doctor, "but I don't see him often these days."

"Oh?" said Mr. Utterson. "I thought you had a number of common interests."

"We once had much in common," said Dr. Lanyon, "but it is more than ten years since Henry Jekyll became too fanciful for me. He began to go wrong in [1] his mind and he spoke such unscientific nonsense that I couldn't bear to listen to him any longer."

"Did you ever come across a friend of his called Hyde?" asked Mr. Utterson.

"Hyde?" repeated Dr. Lanyon. "No. I've never heard of him."

That night, Mr. Utterson's mind was in turmoil and he had little rest. He was haunted by confused dreams about Enfield's shocking story and Jekyll's relationship with his protege, Hyde. When the church bells rang at six the next morning, he was still thinking about the problem. And he became curious to see the features of Edward Hyde. If he could see him just once, he might understand the reason for the unusual conditions of Henry Jekyll's will. And he might know why his friend, Enfield, had immediately hated him.

□ what is on one's mind 하고 싶은 말, 속마음
□ suppose 생각하다, 추정하다
□ common interest 공통의 관심사 (= mutual interest)
□ fanciful 상상(공상)의
□ unscientific 비과학적인
□ nonsense 말도 안 되는 생각(말)

□ bear to + 동사원형 …하는 것을 참다 (견디다)
□ come across 마주치다, 우연히 만나다
□ be in turmoil 혼란에 빠지다
□ be haunted by …에 괴롭힘을 당하다
□ confused 혼란스러운
□ protege 피보호자, 피후견인
□ features 외모

1 **go wrong in one's mind** 정신이 이상해지다
He began to go wrong in his mind. 그는 정신이 이상해지기 시작했다네.

From then on, Mr. Utterson began to watch the door
Mr. Enfield had shown him, and his patience was finally [1]
rewarded at ten o'clock on a fine, frosty night. He had
been watching for some time when he heard light
footsteps on the pavement. He stepped back into the
shadows of the entry to the courtyard.

Moments later, a small, plainly dressed man appeared
and Mr. Utterson immediately experienced a strong [2]
dislike for him. As he approached the door, the man
took a key from his pocket and at that moment, Mr.
Utterson stepped out of the shadows.

"Mr. Hyde, I believe?" said Mr. Utterson, touching the man on his shoulder.

Mr. Hyde did not look around but he answered calmly.

"That's my name. What do you want?"

"I'm an old friend of Dr. Jekyll's and I'm sure you've heard of me," said the lawyer. "My name is Utterson. I thought you might invite me inside."

"You won't find Dr. Jekyll here," said Mr. Hyde.

"I know it," said Utterson, "but I heard that you live here. Will you let me see your face?"

**❓ Who was waiting for Mr. Hyde?**
  a. Mr. Utterson
  b. Mr. Enfield
  c. Dr. Jekyll

---

□ frosty  서리가 내리는, 무척 추운
□ footstep  발자국 소리
□ pavement  인도, 보도
□ step back into  …로 물러서다

□ shadow  어둠, 그늘
□ plainly dressed  수수한 옷차림을 한
□ step out of  …에서 나오다

---

1  **one's patience is rewarded**  …의 인내심이 보상을 받다
His patience was finally rewarded at ten o'clock on a fine, frosty night.  그의 인내심은 맑고 서리가 내리는 밤 열 시에 마침내 보상을 받았다.

2  **experience a strong dislike for**  …에 대해 강한 혐오감을 느끼다
Mr. Utterson immediately experienced a strong dislike for him.
어터슨 씨는 즉시 그에 대해 강한 혐오감을 느꼈다.

Mr. Hyde hesitated briefly before turning to face the lawyer. They stared at each other for a few seconds.

"Now I will recognize you if I see you again," said Mr. Utterson. "It may be useful."

"Yes," said Mr. Hyde, "it's time we met and you should have my address."

He gave the lawyer the number of a house on a street in Soho.* 소호 거리는 런던의 중앙에 위치하고 있으며 식당과 술집들이 많이 모여 있답니다.

"How did you know me?" asked Mr. Hyde.

"By description," said Mr. Utterson. "We have common friends, like Henry Jekyll, for instance."

"Don't lie!" cried Mr. Hyde angrily. "We have no friends in common and Jekyll never told you about me!"

Before the lawyer could answer, Mr. Hyde gave a harsh, savage laugh and disappeared into the house.

□ hesitate 망설이다, 주저하다
□ description 설명, 묘사
□ common friend 공통의 친구
　(= mutual friend)
□ for instance 예를 들면
□ harsh 냉혹한, 가혹한
□ savage 야만적인, 흉포한, 몹시 사나운
□ disappear into … 안으로 사라지다
□ deep in thought 생각에 깊이 잠겨
□ dwarfish (기형적으로) 작은

□ deformed 기형의, 불구의
□ deformity 기형, 불구
□ nasty 불쾌한, 기분 나쁜
□ hatred of (for) … 에 대한 증오심
　(혐오감)
□ narrow 좁은, 협소한
□ square 구역, 지구 (= block)
□ be neglected 방치되다
□ well-dressed 옷 맵시가 단정한,
　좋은 옷을 입은

Mr. Utterson stood for a few minutes after Mr. Hyde left him. He felt anxious but didn't know why. Then he began to slowly walk away down the street, deep in thought. He had finally seen Edward Hyde. The man was pale and dwarfish. He seemed to be deformed, but Mr. Utterson could not see or describe the deformity. Mr. Hyde had a nasty smile and an unpleasant voice, but these things did not explain his immediate hatred of the man.

Around the corner from the narrow street there was a square of old, elegant houses. Many of them were neglected but one house was still in good condition. [1]  Mr. Utterson stopped at the door and knocked. An elderly, well-dressed servant opened the door.

---

1 **be in good condition** 보존 상태가 좋다
Many of them were neglected but one house was still in good condition.
많은 집들이 방치되어 있었지만, 한 집은 여전히 보존 상태가 좋았다.

"Is Dr. Jekyll at home, Poole?" asked the lawyer.

"No sir," said Poole. "Dr. Jekyll is out."

"I saw Mr. Hyde go in by the old laboratory door, Poole," he said. "Is that acceptable, when Dr. Jekyll is not home?"

"Oh, yes," replied the servant. "Mr. Hyde has a key and we have orders to obey him." [1]

"I don't think I've ever met Mr. Hyde," said Mr. Utterson.

"Indeed, we see very little of him in this part of the house," replied the butler. "He generally comes and goes through the laboratory."

Mr. Utterson walked home more worried than ever.

---

□ laboratory 실험실
□ acceptable 허락된, 받아들일 수 있는
□ than ever 여느 때보다도
□ fortnight 2주일
□ lively 활기찬, 생기 있는
□ stay behind 뒤에 남다

□ depart 떠나다, 출발하다
□ approve of …을 허락〔승인〕하다
□ well-built 체격이 좋은, 건장한
□ unnecessarily 불필요하게, 쓸데없이
□ disturbing 마음에 걸리는, 불안감을 주는

1 **have an order to obey** …에게 복종하라는 명령을〔지시를〕 받다
Mr. Hyde has a key and we have orders to obey him.
하이드 씨는 열쇠를 가지고 있고 우리는 그에게 복종하라는 명령을 받았습니다.

2 **arrange to + 동사원형** …하도록 조치를 취하다
Mr. Utterson arranged to stay behind after the others departed.
어터슨 씨는 다른 사람들이 떠난 후에 뒤에 남도록 조치를 취했다.

A fortnight later, Dr. Jekyll invited half-a-dozen old friends to one of his lively dinners. Mr. Utterson arranged to stay behind after the others departed. [2]

"I want to speak to you about your will, Jekyll," said the lawyer. "You know I've never approved of it."

"My friend," said Dr. Jekyll, a large, well-built man of fifty, "you worry unnecessarily."

"Well, I tell you so again," said the lawyer. "I've recently heard something disturbing about Mr. Hyde."

The handsome face of Dr. Jekyll grew pale, and his eyes darkened.

"It doesn't matter what you've heard," he said. "I'm in a strange and terrible situation that can't be altered by talking about it."

"Trust me, Jekyll," said Mr. Utterson. "Tell me about your situation. Your secret is safe with me, whatever it is. And I have no doubt that I can get you out of it."

"My dear friend," said the doctor, "I believe you and I trust you more than any man. I can't tell you what's wrong but I promise you one thing. I can get rid of Hyde whenever I choose. You must understand, however, that I take a great interest in him. And if anything happens to me, please ensure that he gets everything I have left him in my will. It would ease [1] my mind if you would promise to help him."

"I can't pretend that I like him," said the lawyer.

"I don't ask that," said Dr. Jckyll.

He stood up and put his hand on Mr. Utterson's shoulder.

"Help him for my sake, when I'm no longer here," said Dr. Jekyll.

Mr. Utterson sighed deeply.

"I promise," he said.

---

□ darken 어두워지다
□ matter 중요하다
□ be altered by …로 인해 바뀌다
□ whatever it is 그것이 무엇이든
□ have no doubt that절 …을 확신하다, …에 의심의 여지가 없다
□ get A out of B A를 B에서 빼내다

□ get rid of …을 없애다〔제거하다〕
□ take an interest in …에 관심을 가지다
□ ensure that절 …을 확실히 하다
□ pretend that절 …인 척하다
□ for one's sake …을 위해서

1 **ease one's mind** …의 마음을 편하게 해주다, …을 안심시키다
It would ease my mind if you would promise to help him.
자네가 그를 돕겠다고 약속한다면 내 마음을 편하게 해줄 것 같네.

# Check-up Time!



● **WORDS**

단어와 단어의 뜻을 서로 연결하세요.

**1** deformity ・ ・ a. the action of receiving something when someone dies

**2** fanciful ・ ・ b. extremely cruel, violent, and uncontrolled

**3** inheritance ・ ・ c. a condition in which a part of the body is not the normal shape

**4** savage ・ ・ d. unrealistic or unlikely to be true

● **STRUCTURE**

괄호 안의 두 단어 중 맞는 것에 동그라미 하세요.

**1** He immediately experienced a strong dislike (with / for) him.

**2** All his possessions were to pass (into / over) the hands of Edward Hyde.

**3** Mr. Utterson arranged to stay (beyond / behind) after the others departed.

**4** You must understand that I take a great interest (in / to) him.

ANSWERS

**Words |** 1. c  2. d  3. a  4. b
**Structure |** 1. for  2. into  3. behind  4. in

다음은 누가 한 말일까요? 기호를 써넣으세요.

a. 
Mr. Hyde

b. 
Dr. Lanyon

c. 
Mr. Utterson

**1** "We once had much in common." ______

**2** "I want to speak to you about your will." ______

**3** "You won't find Dr. Jekyll here." ______

● SUMMARY

빈칸에 맞는 말을 골라 이야기를 완성하세요.

Mr. Utterson reviewed the conditions of Dr. Jekyll's (     ). It stated that Mr. Hyde would inherit all of Dr. Jekyll's possessions in case of his (     ) or absence. He thought Dr. Jekyll was in trouble and went to see Mr. Hyde, but he didn't get an (     ) from him. A fortnight later, Dr. Jekyll invited Mr. Utterson for dinner. Mr. Utterson was worried about the Dr. Jekyll's (     ) with Mr. Hyde, but Dr. Jekyll wanted to ensure that Mr. Hyde would get everything Dr. Jekyll would have left him.

a. disappearance    b. answer
c. will    d. relationship

ANSWERS

# CHAPTER 3

# The Carew Murder

커루 살인 사건

Nearly a year later, in October, London was startled by the unusually vicious murder of a respected, elderly gentleman. A maid living alone in a house not far from the river witnessed the crime. She was sitting upstairs beside the window about eleven when she noticed the elderly gentleman walking along the lane near the house. Approaching him from the opposite direction was a very small gentleman to whom, at first, she paid no attention. When they met, the older man bowed politely to the small man and seemed to ask for directions. The moon shone on his face and the girl thought he seemed to have a kind and innocent expression.

□ be startled by …에 놀라다
□ vicious 잔혹한, 끔찍한
□ maid 하녀
□ witness 목격하다
□ from the opposite direction
　 반대 방향에서

□ pay no attention 주의를 기울이지
　 않다
□ bow (허리를 굽혀) 인사하다
□ impatiently 못 참겠다는 듯, 조바심내며
□ stamp one's foot 발을 구르다
□ brandish 휘두르다

**1  break out in a flame of anger** 불같이 화를 내다
All of a sudden, he broke out in a great flame of anger.
갑자기, 그는 불같이 화를 냈다.

Then she looked at the other man and was surprised
to recognize him. It was Mr. Hyde, who had once
visited her master. He held a heavy cane in his hand
and appeared to be listening impatiently to the old
man. All of a sudden, he broke out in a great flame of [1]
anger, stamping his foot and brandishing his cane.

The old gentleman took a step back. Mr. Hyde lashed [1] out with his cane and began to beat the old man's body until the girl could hear bones snapping. At the horror of these sights and sounds, she fainted.

It was two o'clock when she came to herself and called for the police. The murderer was gone long ago but his victim lay dead in the middle of the lane, horribly mangled. One shattered half of the cane that had been used to commit this crime was found in the gutter. The murderer had taken the other half. A wallet and a gold watch were found in the dead man's pockets, along with a sealed and stamped envelope. The envelope was [2] addressed to Mr. Utterson.

The letter was brought to the lawyer early the next morning. When he was told about the murder, he turned pale. He drove to the police station where the victim had been carried and as soon as he saw the body, he nodded.

---

1 **take a step back** 한 발짝 뒤로 물러서다
The old gentleman took a step back.
늙은 신사는 한 발짝 뒤로 물러섰다.

2 **be addressed to** (편지 봉투에) …앞으로 주소가 쓰여져 있다
The envelope was addressed to Mr. Utterson.
그 편지 봉투는 어터슨 씨 앞으로 주소가 쓰여져 있었다.

"I recognize him," he said. "I am sorry to say that this is Sir Danvers Carew."

"Good God, sir!" exclaimed the police officer. "Well, perhaps you can help us find the man who did this to him."

And he briefly narrated what the maid had seen, and showed the lawyer the broken cane.

Mr. Utterson had felt a twinge of anxiety when he heard Hyde's name. But when he saw the cane, he knew the maid had been right. Although the cane was broken, he recognized it as one he had given to Henry Jekyll many years ago.

"Come with me," said Mr. Utterson to the police officer, "I think I know where Mr. Hyde lives."

❓ Which is not the object in the dead man's pockets?
ㄴ a. gold watch    b. sealed envelope    c. half of the cane

정답 ㄱ

□ lash out with  ···로 후려치다 〔강타하다〕
□ beat  (아주 세게) 치다, 때리다 (beat-beat-beaten)
□ snap  딱하고 부러지다
□ faint  기절하다, 정신을 잃다
□ come to oneself  정신을 차리다
□ murderer  살인자
□ lie + 형용사  ···인 채 누워 있다 (lie-lay-lain)

□ lane  골목길
□ mangled  뭉개진, 심하게 훼손된
□ shattered  박살난, 부서진
□ commit a crime  범죄를 저지르다
□ gutter  배수로, 하수구
□ sealed  봉해진
□ victim  피해자, 희생자
□ exclaim  소리치다, 외치다
□ narrate  설명하다, (이야기)를 들려주다
□ a twinge of anxiety  격렬한 불안감

The address in Soho was in a dingy street where ragged children crouched in doorways and poorly dressed women haggled with storekeepers outside dirty shops. [1] This was where Henry Jekyll's young friend lived. Mr. Utterson shuddered. Mr. Hyde was heir to a quarter of a million pounds.

1 **haggle with** (물건값을 깎으려고) …와 실랑이를 벌이다
Poorly dressed women haggled with storekeepers outside dirty shops. 허름한 옷차림의 여자들이 지저분한 가게 밖에서 주인들과 물건값을 깎으려고 실랑이를 벌이고 있었다.

A silver-haired old woman opened the door. She had an evil face, but her manners were polite. She told them that Mr. Hyde lived there but he was not at home. Until yesterday, she had not seen him for nearly two months.

"This gentleman with me is Inspector Newcomen of Scotland Yard," said Mr. Utterson. "We would like to see Mr. Hyde's rooms."

영국 런던 경찰국의 별칭으로 1829년 창설 당시 위치가 런던의 옛 스코틀랜드 국왕의 궁전터였기 때문에 이런 별칭을 얻게 되었답니다.

Mr. Hyde had only two rooms in the house but they were furnished with good taste. A cupboard was filled with fine wine, and beautiful pictures hung on the walls. Mr. Utterson supposed they were gifts from Henry Jekyll, who was a lover of fine art. Clothes lay about the floor of the room and cupboard doors hung open. In the fireplace, the inspector found part of a checkbook among a pile of grey ashes. Behind the door he discovered the missing half of the broken cane.

□ dingy 우중충한, 지저분한
□ ragged 누더기를 걸친
□ crouch 웅크리다
□ doorway 출입구, 문
□ shudder (공포나 추위로) 몸을 떨다
□ heir to …의 상속인
□ inspector 경감
□ Scotland Yard (영국의) 런던 경찰국
□ furnished 가구가 비치된

□ taste 취향
□ cupboard 찬장, 벽장
□ hang (그림 등이 벽에) 걸려 있다
 (hang - hung - hung)
□ fine art 미술
□ lie about …에 흩어져 있다
□ hang open 열려 젖혀져 있다
□ checkbook 수표책
□ pile 더미, 무더기

"Excellent! We will catch him soon," he told Mr.
Utterson. "Now let's visit the bank and see if they can
tell us anything about the owner of this checkbook."

Sure enough, the bank held several thousand pounds
in an account in the name of Edward Hyde.

"We have him now," said the inspector. "We've got
the murder weapon and we've got this checkbook.
Why, money's life to the man. We have nothing to do
but wait for him to visit the bank. Now we only need
his image and description on the Wanted posters."

It proved impossible, however, to get a picture of Hyde for the posters. The man had never been photographed. The few people who tried to describe him couldn't agree on his features although all concurred that he was somehow deformed. But when they were asked to describe Hyde's deformity, none could do it.

Later that afternoon, Mr. Utterson went to Dr. Jekyll's house. He was greeted by Poole who showed him into the doctor's office. Dr. Jekyll sat beside the fire, looking deadly sick. He held out a cold hand to his friend and welcomed him in a weak voice.

□ see if〔whether〕 …인지 (아닌지)
□ sure enough 물론 말할 것도 없이
□ account 계좌
□ murder weapon 살해 도구
□ have nothing to do but + 동사원형
　 …하기만 하면 된다
□ Wanted poster 수배 전단지

□ be photographed 사진을 찍히다
□ agree on …에 대해 동의하다
□ concur that절 …에 동의하다
　 (concur - concurred - concurred)
□ be greeted by …의 환영을 받다
□ hold out a hand to …에게 손을 내밀다

### Mini-Less⚙n

**to 부정사의 의미상의 주어**

to 부정사의 주어가 문장 전체의 주어와 일치하지 않을 때는 to 부정사 앞에 「for + 명사〔대명사〕」를 써서 to 부정사의 주어를 밝혀준답니다.

- We have nothing to do but wait for him to visit the bank.
  우리는 그가 은행을 방문하는 것을 기다리기만 하면 됩니다.
- It was very hard for him to lose weight.  그가 살을 빼는 것은 무척 힘든 일이었다.

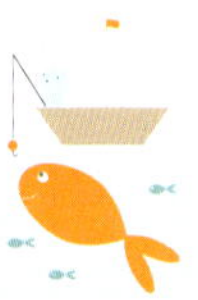

"Have you heard the news?" asked Mr. Utterson, when they were alone.

"Yes, the newsboys were crying it in the square," said Dr. Jekyll.

"Tell me, you have not been mad enough to hide this fellow?" asked Mr. Utterson.

"I swear to God I will never set eyes on him again," said the doctor. "I bind my honor to you that I'm done [1] with him. He's gone and will never be heard of again."

"You seem pretty sure of him," said Mr. Utterson, "and I hope you may be right. If it came to a trial, your name might be mentioned."

<br>

- □ newsboy 신문 배달원
- □ fellow 친구, 녀석
- □ swear to God 신에게 맹세하다
- □ set eyes on …을 만나다
- □ be done with …와 끝나다〔다시는 만나지 않다〕
- □ come to a trial 재판을 받다
- □ have grounds for …에 대한 근거가 있다
- □ certainty 확신, 확실함
- □ share with …와 공유하다
- □ judge 판단하다, 짐작하다
- □ have trust in …을 믿다〔신뢰하다〕
- □ odd 특이한, 독특한
- □ upright 똑바른
- □ benefactor 후원자, 은인
- □ generosity 관대함, 자비로움
- □ repay …에 보답하다

1 **bind A's honor to B** B에게 A의 명예를 걸고 약속하다
I bind my honor to you that I'm done with him.
그와의 관계가 끝났다는 것을 자네에게 내 명예를 걸고 약속하겠네.

2 **leave A in B's hands** A를 B에게 맡기다〔일임하다〕
I'd like to leave it in your hands, Utterson.
나는 이것을 자네에게 맡기고 싶네, 어터슨.

"I am quite sure of him," said Dr. Jekyll. "I have grounds for certainty that I cannot share with anyone. But there is one thing on which you may advise me. I received a letter and I don't know if I should show it to the police. I'd like to leave it in your hands, Utterson. [2] You would judge wisely and I have such great trust in you."

"Let me see the letter," said Mr. Utterson.

It was written in an odd, upright style, and signed "Edward Hyde." It was brief and said that his friend and benefactor, Dr. Jekyll, need not worry about him. He was safe and would never be found and he thanked Dr. Jekyll for his generosity, which he could never repay.

"Do you have the envelope?" asked Mr. Utterson.

"I burned it without thinking," replied Dr. Jekyll, "but it bore no postmark. The note was handed in."

"Shall I keep this and sleep on it?" asked Mr. Utterson.

"Please do. I wish you to judge it entirely for me," said Dr. Jekyll. "I have lost confidence in myself." [1]

"I will consider it," said the lawyer. "And one more question. Was it Hyde who dictated the conditions in your will about your disappearance?"

Dr. Jekyll shut his mouth tight and nodded.

"I knew it," said Mr. Utterson. "He meant to murder you. You have had a narrow escape."

"I have had what is far more to the purpose," said the doctor, solemnly. "I have had a lesson. Oh God, Utterson! What a lesson I have had!"

And he covered his face for a moment with his hands.

---

□ bear 붙어 있다 (bear – bore – borne)
□ postmark (우편물의) 소인
□ be handed in 인편으로 건네지다
□ sleep on ⋯에 대해 하룻밤 자면서 생각하다
□ dictate 명령하다
□ mean to + 동사원형 ⋯하려고 의도하다
□ have a narrow escape 구사일생으로 살다
□ be far more to the purpose 훨씬 중요하다
□ solemnly 엄숙하게
□ What + a/an + 명사! 얼마나 대단한 ⋯인지!
□ on one's way out ⋯가 나가는 길에
□ postman 우편배달부
□ either A or B A이거나 B이거나

On his way out, the lawyer stopped and spoke with
Poole.

"There was a letter handed in today for your master,"
he said. "What was the messenger like?"

"Nobody came except the postman, sir," said Poole
in surprise.

Mr. Utterson's fears immediately returned. Either the
letter had been delivered to the laboratory door, or it
had been written in the office and left there for Jekyll.

1 **lose confidence in** ···에 대한 신뢰를 잃다
I have lost confidence in myself.
나는 내 자신에 대한 신뢰를 잃었다네.

- □ call out 외치다
- □ headline (신문의) 머리기사
- □ special edition 호외
- □ get caught up in …에 휘말리다
- □ cross one's mind 생각이 스치다
- □ precisely 정확하게, 신중하게
- □ head clerk 사무장, 서기장
- □ implicitly 절대적으로, 무조건적으로
- □ keep A from B B에게 A를 숨기다
- □ handwriting 필체, 필사본

As Mr. Utterson left Dr. Jekyll's house, he heard the newsboys calling out the headlines along the streets: "Special edition! Read all about the vicious murder of Sir Danvers Carew!"

"What a sad and shocking end to the life of my good friend, Sir Danvers," thought Mr. Utterson. "I only pray that Dr. Jekyll does not get caught up in the scandal. But what am I to do about the letter?"

No sooner had the thought crossed his mind than he knew precisely who would be able to answer that question for him.

That evening Mr. Utterson was sitting beside his own fireplace with his head clerk, Mr. Guest. Mr. Utterson trusted Mr. Guest implicitly and kept few secrets from him. Mr. Guest's hobby was the study of handwriting.

---

## Mini-Lesson

### No sooner ... than ~ : …하자마자 ~하다

'…하자마자 ~하다' 라는 표현을 하고 싶을 때는 「No sooner + 동사 + 주어 + than + 주어 + 동사」를 써요. 강조를 위해 No sooner가 문두에 오면서 어순이 도치되어 동사가 주어 앞에 놓였다는 점, 꼭 기억해 두세요.

- No sooner had the thought crossed his mind than he knew precisely who would be able to answer that question for him.  그 생각이 스치자마자 그는 그 질문에 대답을 할 수 있는 사람이 누구인지 정확하게 알았다.
- No sooner was Mr. Utterson alone that night than he locked the note into his safe. 그날 밤 어터슨 씨가 혼자 있게 되자마자 금고 안에 편지를 넣고 잠갔다.

"This is a sad business about Sir Danvers," said
Mr. Utterson.

"It is, sir. It has elicited a great deal of public feeling,"
said Guest. "The man who did it is mad, of course."

"I would like to hear your views on that," said
Mr. Utterson. "I have a document here in the
murderer's handwriting. Please read it and, of course,
this is entirely between ourselves." [1]

Mr. Guest's eyes brightened, and he sat down at once
and studied the letter with passion.

"Well, sir," he said at last, "the man is not mad, but it
is very odd writing."

Just then, Mr. Utterson's servant entered, carrying
a note for his master.

"Is that from Dr. Jekyll, sir?" asked Mr. Guest.
"I thought I knew the writing. Is it private?"

---

☐ elicit 끌어내다
☐ public feeling 민심, 동정
☐ entirely 전적으로
☐ with passion 열정적으로
☐ private 사적인, 비공개의
☐ content (문서의) 내용

☐ identical 동일한, 같은
☐ hand 필체, 서체
☐ slope to …로 비스듬히 기울다
☐ speak of …에 대해 발설하다
☐ lock A into B A를 B에 넣고 잠그다
☐ forge 위조하다

1 **be between ourselves** 우리 사이의 일로 하다
   Please read it and, of course, this is entirely between ourselves.
   이것을 읽어보게 그리고, 물론 이것은 우리 사이의 일로 해야 하네.

"No, it's only an invitation to dinner," said Mr. Utterson. "Do you want to see it?"

"Just for a moment," said Mr. Guest.

He laid the two [2] sheets of paper beside each other and compared their contents.

"Well, sir," he said at last, "the writing is very similar in both notes. Many things about them are identical, except that one hand slopes to the right and the other is upright."

"That's extremely odd," said Mr. Utterson. "I wouldn't speak of this, Mr. Guest."

"I understand, sir," said the clerk.

But no sooner was Mr. Utterson alone that night than he locked the note into his safe.

"Why would Henry Jekyll forge a letter for a murderer?" he wondered.

And fear made his blood run cold.

---

[2] **lay ... beside each other**  …을 나란히 놓다
He laid the two sheets of paper beside each other and compared their contents.  그는 두 장의 종이를 나란히 놓고 내용을 비교했다.

# Check-up Time!

● **WORDS**

빈칸에 알맞은 단어를 보기에서 골라 써넣으세요.

| startled    greeted    addressed    furnished |
| --- |

**1** The envelope was __________ to Mr. Utterson.

**2** Mr. Hyde's rooms were __________ with good taste.

**3** He went to Dr. Jekyll's house and was __________ by Poole who showed him into the doctor's office.

**4** London was __________ by the vicious murder of a gentleman.

● **STRUCTURE**

빈칸에 알맞은 형태의 단어를 골라 문장을 완성하세요.

**1** Mr. Hyde meant to __________ you.
a. murdered          b. murder          c. murdering

**2** We have nothing to do but __________ for him to visit the bank.
a. wait          b. waiting          c. to wait

**3** I bind my honor to you that I'm __________ with him.
a. do          b. doing          c. done

다음 질문에 알맞은 답을 고르세요.

**1** How did the maid recognize Mr. Hyde as the murderer of Sir Danvers Carew?

   a. She had seen him when he visited her master before.

   b. She had once collided with him at night.

**2** What did the inspector find in Hyde's room?

   a. He found a picture of Hyde on the wall.

   b. He found part of a checkbook in the fireplace.

● **SUMMARY**

빈칸에 맞는 말을 골라 이야기를 완성하세요.

A year later, a vicious murder (　　). A well-known man, Sir Danvers was killed by Mr. Hyde. The police and Mr. Utterson tried to find him, but they (　　). That afternoon, Mr. Utterson went to Dr. Jekyll's house to ask about Mr. Hyde, and Dr. Jekyll gave him a letter from Mr. Hyde. That evening, Mr. Utterson looked through the letter with his (　　), and they found out that there were some similarities between the (　　) of Dr. Jekyll and that of Mr. Hyde.

a. handwritings      b. head clerk

c. failed      d. occurred

Comprehension | 1. a  2. b    Summary | d, c, b, a

# Soho in London

런던의 소호

Soho is a district of central London, in the City of Westminster. The area was a farmland until 1536, when it was taken by King Henry VIII as a royal park. The name "Soho" first appears in the 17th century and most people believe that the name derives from a former hunting cry "So-ho." Despite this royal attention and grand development taking place in neighboring districts, Soho never became a fashionable area for the rich and was mostly known as an area settled by new

immigrants. By the mid-19th century it had become a haven for cheap pubs and restaurants. Things got better in the early 1900s when it gained something of a Bohemian reputation with writers, artists, and actors moving in. In the 1950s the music business began to prosper and since the 1980s, the whole Soho area has undergone rapid transformation and development into a fashion district. Now Soho is a multicultural area of central London; a home to industry, commerce, culture and entertainment and represents the vibrant, bustling heart of the city.

소호는 시티 오브 웨스트민스터 내에 있는 런던 중심부 지역입니다. 이 지역은 1536년 헨리 8세가 왕실 공원으로 사용하기 전까지는 농지였습니다. '소호'라는 이름은 17세기에 처음 등장했는데 대부분의 사람들은 소호라는 이름이 예전에 사냥할 때 외치던 말인 '소-호'에서 나왔다고 믿고 있습니다. 왕의 관심과 주변 지역들에서 진행된 대규모의 개발 사업에도 불구하고, 소호는 부자들을 위한 상류층의 장소가 되지 못했고 주로 새로운 이민자들이 정착한 곳으로만 알려져 있었습니다. 19세기 중반까지 소호는 저렴한 술집과 식당들이 자리잡기에 좋은 곳이 되었습니다. 1900년대 초반에 작가와 예술가, 배우들이 모여들면서 보헤미안들이 사는 지역이라는 명성을 얻으면서 상황이 나아졌습니다. 1950년대에는 음악 산업이 번성하기 시작했고, 1980년대부터 소호 지역 전체가 급격한 변화와 개발을 겪으며 패션 지구로 거듭났습니다. 오늘날의 소호는 런던 중심부의 다문화 지역으로 산업, 상업, 문화, 오락의 중심지이자 활기차고 사람들이 북적이는 도심을 대표하고 있습니다.

# CHAPTER 4

# The Death of Dr. Lanyon

래니언 박사의 죽음

Thousands of pounds were offered as a reward for the capture of the murderer of Sir Danvers. Stories were told of Hyde's cruelty, his vile life, and his strange associates, but no trace was found of him. He had disappeared as if he had never existed.

As time passed, Mr. Utterson began to recover from the fever of his alarming discoveries and to grow more at peace with himself. The death of Sir Danvers was, to [1] his way of thinking, more than paid for by the disappearance of Mr. Hyde.

For Dr. Jekyll, a new life began. He renewed old friendships and became once more a familiar and welcome guest. For more than two months, Mr. Utterson saw him every day and knew that the doctor was also in a state of inner harmony.

---

1 **be more than paid for by** …로 충분히 보상을 받다
The death of Sir Danvers was, to his way of thinking, more than paid for by the disappearance of Mr. Hyde.
댄버스 경의 죽음은, 그의 생각으로는, 하이드 씨의 실종으로 충분히 보상을 받았다.

On the 8th of January, Mr. Utterson dined at Dr. Jekyll's. Dr. Lanyon was there too and it was like the old days when the three men had been inseparable.

But on the 12th and again on the 14th, Dr. Jekyll shut his doors against the lawyer.

"The doctor is confined to the house," said Poole.

Mr. Utterson became increasingly concerned when this pattern continued for the next two days.

□ be offered as …로 내걸리다
□ reward 현상금, 보상금
□ capture 검거, 포획
□ cruelty 잔인함, 잔혹함
□ vile 극도로 불쾌한(나쁜)
□ associate 동료
□ trace 흔적, 실마리
□ recover from …에서 회복되다
□ alarming 걱정스러운, 두려운
□ grow at peace with oneself
　　마음이 평온해지다

□ to one's way of thinking …의
　　생각으로는
□ renew 재개하다, 되살리다
□ in a state of …의 상태인
□ inner 내면의, 내부의
□ harmony 조화, 화합
□ inseparable (사람 사이를) 갈라 놓을
　　수 없는
□ shut A's door against B  A의
　　문을 B에게 닫다
□ be confined to …에 틀어박혀 있다

### Mini-Lesson

See p. 128

**as if + 가정법 과거완료(had + p.p.)**: 마치 …했던 것처럼

as if 다음에 가정법 과거완료, 즉 「had + p.p.」가 오면 주절보다 더 전에 일어난 사실을 가정하는 표현이 만들어져 '마치 …했던 것처럼'이라는 뜻이 된답니다.

• He had disappeared as if he had never existed.
　그는 마치 원래 존재하지 않았던 것처럼 사라졌다.
• She treats me as if she had seen me before.
　그녀는 마치 전에 나를 본 적이 있었던 것처럼 대한다.

At the end of that week, he visited Dr. Lanyon and was welcomed as always, but he was shocked at the change that had taken place in his friend's appearance. Dr. Lanyon had grown pale and thin in just a few days and he was visibly older and balder. He looked like a man close to death. But when Mr. Utterson asked about his health, Dr. Lanyon spoke without fear.

"I've had a shock," said Dr. Lanyon frankly, "and I will never recover. It is just a matter of time. My life has been pleasant and I used to enjoy it."

"Jekyll is ill, too," said Mr. Utterson. "Have you seen him?"

Dr. Lanyon's face changed and he held up a trembling hand.

"I wish to see or hear no more of Jekyll," he said, in an unsteady voice. "I am quite done with him and I beg that you spare me any allusion to one whom I regard [1] as dead."

"Oh, dear," said Mr. Utterson. "We are three very old friends, Lanyon. We won't live to make others."

"Nothing can be done," said Dr. Lanyon. "Ask him."

"He won't let me into the house," said Mr. Utterson.

"That doesn't surprise me," said the doctor. "Some day, after I'm dead, you will come to learn the right and wrong of this. Please don't talk about that man. I can't bear it."

□ take place  일어나다, 발생하다
□ visibly  눈에 띄게, 분명히
□ bald  대머리의, 머리가 벗겨진
□ close to death  죽음이 임박한
□ without fear  두려움 없이
□ frankly  솔직하게
□ a matter of time  (곧 일어나게 될) 시간의 문제

□ used to ＋ 동사원형  (과거에) …했다
□ trembling  떨리는
□ unsteady  불안정한, 떨리는
□ allusion to  …에 대한 언급〔암시〕
□ regard A as B  A를 B로 간주하다
□ let ... into  …을 안으로 들이다
□ come to ＋ 동사원형  …하게 되다

1  spare A B  A가 B를 하지 않도록 하다
   I beg that you spare me any allusion to one whom I regard as dead.  내가 죽었다고 간주하는 사람에 대한 언급을 하지 않도록 해주게.

As soon as he got home, Mr. Utterson sat down
and wrote to Dr. Jekyll. In his letter he asked why
Dr. Jekyll refused to let him into his house and why he
and Dr. Lanyon were no longer friendly.

The next day, he received Dr. Jekyll's reply.

"The quarrel with Lanyon is irreparable," wrote
Dr. Jekyll. "I don't blame him, but I share his view that
we must never meet. I intend to lead a solitary life [1]
from now on. You must not be surprised, nor must you ☀
doubt my friendship, if my door is shut even to you.
My own actions have put me in terrible danger and
I am being punished for them. I can tell you nothing
except that I am suffering for my sins. Please respect
my silence. You can do nothing for me."

---

[1] **lead a solitary life** 고독한 삶을 살다
I intend to lead a solitary life from now on.
나는 이제부터 계속 고독한 삶을 살 생각이네.

### Mini-Less☀n

부정문, nor + (조)동사 + 주어: …도 ~하지 않다
nor이 부정문 뒤에 쓰이면 부정의 연속을 나타내어 '…도 ~하지 않다'는 뜻이 되며,
nor 뒤에는 「(조)동사 + 주어」로 어순이 도치된답니다.

• You must not be surprised, nor must you doubt my friendship, if my door is shut
  even to you.  만약 내 집 문이 자네한테마저 굳게 닫힌다 해도 놀라지 말고 내 우정도 의심하지 말게나.
• She doesn't like Sam, nor does Chris.  그녀는 샘을 좋아하지 않고, 크리스도 좋아하지 않는다.

A few weeks later, Dr. Lanyon took his bed and in less than a fortnight he was dead. The night after the funeral, Mr. Utterson took a sealed envelope from his private safe. Written across it in Dr. Lanyon's handwriting were the words, *"PRIVATE. To be opened only by G. J. Utterson."*

The lawyer broke the seal. Another sealed envelope was inside. On it was written *"Not to be opened till the death or disappearance of Dr. Henry Jekyll."*

□ refuse to + 동사원형 …하는 것을
　거절하다
□ irreparable  회복할〔바로잡을〕수 없는
□ intend to + 동사원형 …할 생각이다
□ put ... in danger …을 위험에
　빠뜨리다
□ be punished for …때문에 벌
　〔처벌〕을 받다
□ sin  죄, 잘못
□ take one's bed  병석에 눕다
□ funeral  장례식
□ seal  (편지 등의) 봉랍

Mr. Utterson was astounded. The same words were in the mad will that he had long since returned to Dr. Jekyll. But what had Dr. Lanyon meant by those words? What had he known? The lawyer was curious and wanted nothing more than to open the letter and [1] solve these mysteries. But his professional honor and his promise to his dead friend were too strong. The envelope would stay in his private safe until the conditions were met.

On their Sunday walk a few weeks later, Mr. Utterson and Mr. Enfield found themselves once more in the small street where they had both met Mr. Hyde.

"Well," said Mr. Enfield, "that story's at an end, at least. We won't see Mr. Hyde again."

"I hope not," said Mr. Utterson. "Did I tell you that I once saw him and shared your feelings of repulsion?"

"It was impossible not to hate him," said Mr. Enfield. "But didn't you think I was stupid not to know that the door is the back entrance to Dr. Jekyll's?"

---

1 **want nothing more than to + 동사원형** 무엇보다 …하고 싶다
The lawyer was curious and wanted nothing more than to open the letter and solve these mysteries. 변호사는 호기심이 생겼고 무엇보다 그 편지를 열어서 이러한 의문들을 해결하고 싶었다.

- astounded 깜짝 놀란
- long since 오래 전에
- solve a mystery 의문을 해결하다
- professional 직업적인
- conditions are met 조건이 충족되다
- be at an end 끝이 나다, 마무리가 지어지다
- repulsion 혐오감, 역겨움
- back entrance to …로 가는 뒷문

"So you found it out, did you?" said Mr. Utterson.
"But if that is so, we may go into the courtyard and
take a look at the windows. I am uneasy about poor
Jekyll and even outside I feel as if the presence of a
friend might do him good."

Although the street was bright and sunny, the courtyard was damp and full of shadows. The middle window of Dr. Jekyll's office was halfway open and he was sitting beside it. His face wore the sad expression of a prisoner who longs for freedom. [1]

"Jekyll!" cried Mr. Utterson. "What a surprise! I hope you're feeling better."

"I'm very low," replied Dr. Jekyll. "It won't last long, thank God."

"You stay indoors too much," said the lawyer. "You should be outside getting some exercise. Come on, get your hat and walk with us for a while."

"I would like to but it's impossible," said Dr. Jekyll. "I'm glad to see you, though, Utterson. I'd invite you and Mr. Enfield in but the place is not fit."

□ be uneasy about ···에 대해 불안 하다〔걱정되다〕
□ presence 존재
□ do ... good ···에게 도움〔이득〕이 되다
□ damp 습기 찬, 축축한
□ halfway 반쯤, 중간까지

□ wear (어떤 표정을) 짓고 있다
□ low (몸이나 기분이) 처지는, 기운이 없는
□ last 지속〔계속〕되다
□ invite ... in ···을 안으로 초대하다
□ fit 적당한, 적합한

1 long for ···을 갈망〔소망〕하다
His face wore the sad expression of a prisoner who longs for freedom. 그의 얼굴은 자유를 갈망하는 죄수의 슬픈 표정을 짓고 있었다.

"Well then, why don't we just stay down here and speak with you?" said Mr. Utterson.

"I was about to venture to suggest the very same [1] thing," said the doctor, with a faint smile.

But he had hardly finished speaking when his smile was replaced with an expression of terror and despair. [2] Mr. Utterson and Mr. Enfield saw his face only for a moment before the window was slammed shut, but that glimpse was enough to frighten them. They turned and walked quickly away, and only when they had left the street far behind them did Mr. Utterson speak.

"God help us!" he said, with an expression of dread in his eyes.

But Mr. Enfield was still too horrified to speak and only nodded as he walked on in silence.

**?** Dr. Jekyll's __________ was replaced with the expression of terror and despair.

정답 smile

□ **be about to + 동사원형** 막 …하려는 참이다
□ **faint** 희미한, 약한
□ **hardly A when B** A하자마자 B하다
□ **be slammed shut** (문이) 세게 닫히다
□ **glimpse** 힐끗 보기
□ **dread** 두려움, 공포
□ **be horrified** 공포에 떨다, 겁에 질리다
□ **in silence** 조용히, 말없이

**1  venture to + 동사원형**  (조심스럽게) …하다

I was about to venture to suggest the very same thing.
나도 막 똑같은 것을 제안하려던 참이었네.

**2  be replaced with**  …로 바뀌다 [대체되다]

His smile was replaced with an expression of terror and despair.
그의 미소는 공포와 절망의 표정으로 바뀌었다.

## Mini-Lesson

See p. 129

**도치: only + 부사(절/구) + do동사/조동사 + 주어 + 동사원형**

「only + 부사(절/구)」를 강조하기 위해 문두에 둘 때 그 뒤는 어순이 도치되어
「do동사/조동사 + 주어 + 동사원형」이 된답니다.

- Only when they had left the street far behind them did Mr. Utterson speak.
  그들이 그 거리에서 한참 멀어지고 나서야 어터슨 씨는 입을 열었다.
- Only after two hours could she realize the situation.
  두 시간이 지나서야 그녀는 상황을 파악할 수 있었다.

# Check-up Time!



## ● WORDS

단어와 단어의 뜻을 서로 연결하세요.

1 last •     • a. a person who is closely connected with, especially at work

2 allusion •     • b. to begin something again

3 associate •     • c. to continue for a particular period of time

4 renew •     • d. an incidental mention of something, either directly or by implication

## ● STRUCTURE

빈칸에 알맞은 전치사를 보기에서 골라 문장을 완성하세요.

| from | to | for | about | as |
| --- | --- | --- | --- | --- |

1 The doctor is confined __________ the house.

2 I am uneasy __________ poor Jekyll.

3 Mr. Utterson began to recover __________ the fever.

4 Thousands of pounds were offered __________ a reward.

5 His face wore the sad expression of a prisoner who longs __________ freedom.

ANSWERS

Structure | 1. to  2. about  3. from  4. as  5. for
Words | 1. c  2. d  3. a  4. b

다음은 누가 한 말일까요? 기호를 써넣으세요.

a.

Mr. Utterson

b.

Dr. Lanyon

c.
Mr. Enfield

**1** "It was impossible not to hate him."  ________

**2** "I wish to see or hear no more of Jekyll."  ________

**3** "What a surprise! I hope you're feeling better."  ________

● SUMMARY

빈칸에 맞는 말을 골라 이야기를 완성하세요.

As time passed after the murder of (    ), Mr. Utterson's life returned to normal. But after spending some enjoyable time with his friends, (    ) shut his doors again. A few weeks later, (    ) died and left a letter for Mr. Utterson. One Sunday, Mr. Utterson and (    ) walked to Dr. Jekyll's house and saw him. At first, Dr. Jekyll seemed to be fine, but then they saw the dramatic change of his expression and were shocked.

a.  Sir Danvers

b.  Dr. Jekyll

c.  Mr. Enfield

d.  Dr. Lanyon

ANSWERS

Comprehension | 1. c   2. b   3. a
Summary | a, b, d, c

# CHAPTER 5

# The Last Night
마지막 밤

One evening, Mr. Utterson received a visit from Poole.

"Good Heavens, Poole, what brings you here?" he said. "Is the doctor ill?"

"Mr. Utterson," said Poole, "there is something wrong."

"Sit down and let me pour you a glass of wine," said the lawyer. "Take your time, and tell me what has happened."

"You know the doctor's ways, sir," said Poole, "and how he shuts himself up. Now he's shut up in his [1] study. I'm afraid, sir, and I can't bear it any longer."

"Tell me exactly what you're afraid of," said Mr. Utterson.

Poole had not once looked at the lawyer's face. His eyes stared at the floor.

"Come," said Mr. Utterson. "I can see that something is seriously wrong. Tell me what it is."

"I think there's been foul play," said Poole, hoarsely.

"Foul play!" cried the lawyer. "What do you mean?"

"I can't tell you, sir," said Poole, "but will you come with me and see for yourself?"

 Why did Poole visit Mr. Utterson?
a. To shut Mr. Utterson up in his study
b. To drink a glass of wine with Mr. Utterson
c. To talk with Mr. Utterson about his master

□ Good Heavens 이런, 어머　　　　□ study 서재
□ pour A B  A에게 B를 따라주다　　□ foul play 살인, 폭행치사
□ take one's time 천천히 하다　　　□ hoarsely 쉰 목소리로
□ shut oneself up 스스로를 차단시키다　□ for oneself 직접

1 **be shut up in**  …에 틀어박히다
Now he's shut up in his study. 지금 박사님은 서재에 틀어박혀 계십니다.

An expression of relief appeared in the butler's face when Mr. Utterson went to get his hat and coat. It was a wild, windy night with a pale moon that seemed to have swept the streets unusually bare of people.

When they reached Dr. Jekyll's house, Poole knocked lightly on the door. It opened a little on a safety chain.

"Is that you, Poole?" said a voice.

"Yes," said Poole. "Open the door."

They entered the brightly lit hall where a fire blazed in the hearth. All of the servants were gathered there.

At the sight of Mr. Utterson, the cook cried, "Bless God! It's Mr. Utterson."

"Why you are here?" said the lawyer.

"They're all afraid," said Poole.

Blank silence followed until the maid began to weep loudly.

"Be quiet," said Poole, angrily.

□ relief 안도, 안심
□ sweep (거칠게) 휩쓸고 지나가다
   (sweep-swept-swept)
□ bare of ···이 없는
□ on a safety chain 안전 사슬이 걸린 채
□ brightly lit 환하게 불이 켜진
□ blaze 활활 타다
□ hearth 벽난로, 화로

□ be gathered 모여 있다
□ Bless God! 하느님 감사합니다!
□ weep 울다, 눈물을 흘리다
   (weep-wept-wept)
□ lead+사람(A)+to+장소(B) A를 B로 데려가다(안내하다) (lead-led-led)
□ as+형용사+as+주어+can ···가 할 수 있는 한 가장 ~한

And then he led Mr. Utterson to the back garden.

"Please be as quiet as you can, sir," he said. "I want you to hear but not be heard. If he sees you and asks you to go in, don't go."

### Mini-Lesson

**to have + p.p. :** 완료부정사

It was a wild, windy night with a pale moon that seemed to have swept the streets unusually bare of people. (바람이 거세게 불고 달빛이 어슴푸레하게 비치는 밤이었고 평소와는 달리 바람이 휩쓸고 지나간 것처럼 거리에는 사람들이 거의 없었다.) 에서 to have swept는 완료부정사로 본동사 seemed보다 앞서 일어난 일을 나타낸답니다.

• She appears to have completed the project yesterday.
  그녀는 어제 그 프로젝트를 끝낸 것처럼 보인다.

Mr. Utterson followed the butler into the laboratory building. At the foot of the stairs that led to the office, they stopped. Then Poole went up the steps and knocked on the door.

"Mr. Utterson is asking to see you, sir," he called.

"Tell him I can't see anyone," said a plaintive voice.

"Thank you, sir," said Poole and he led Mr. Utterson back across the yard and into the kitchen.

"Well sir," he said, looking Mr. Utterson in the eyes, "was that my master's voice?"

"It seems much changed," replied the lawyer.

"Changed?" said the butler. "I have worked for twenty years in this house. I know my master's voice and the voice in his office is not his. He disappeared eight days ago. We heard him cry out in the name of God and we have not heard him since. The creature in the office also calls for God's mercy!"

---

□ foot of the stairs 계단의 맨 아랫부분
□ plaintive 애처로운, 구슬픈
□ cry out in the name of God 하느님을 부르며 소리치다
□ creature 생명이 있는 존재, 생물
□ mercy 자비
□ commend oneself to reason 납득이 가다

□ night and day 밤낮으로
□ wholesale 도매의, 대량의
□ chemist 약제사, 약사
□ instruct＋목적어(A)＋to＋동사(B) A에게 B할 것을 지시하다
□ impure 불순물이 섞인
□ place an order to …에게 주문을 하다
□ firm 회사

"This is very strange," said Mr. Utterson. "If Dr. Jekyll has been murdered, why would the murderer stay? It doesn't commend itself to reason."

"Well, Mr. Utterson," said Poole. "For a week, the creature in that room has been crying night and day for some drug. The master occasionally wrote his orders on a sheet of paper and left it on the stairs for me. But this week there are notes every day and the door is always closed. I have been to all the wholesale chemists in town and brought back the drug he ordered. Each time, a note instructed me to return the drug because it is impure, and to place an order to a different firm. The creature wants that drug badly, sir."

"Do you have any of these notes?" asked Mr. Utterson.

Poole pulled a crumpled note from his pocket and gave it to the lawyer. Mr. Utterson read:

> *To Messrs Maw, with the compliments of Dr. Jekyll.[1] The last sample is not pure. Some years ago, Dr. Jekyll purchased a large quantity from you. Please look again with more care and if any of the same quality is found, send it to him at once. The cost is unimportant. Dr. Jekyll urgently needs this drug. For God's sake, find me some of the old drug.*



"This is a strange note," said Mr. Utterson. "How do you come to have it open?"

"The man at Maw's was angry and threw it back to me," said Poole.

"This is unquestionably Dr. Jekyll's handwriting, isn't it?" said the lawyer.

"I thought so," said Poole. "But why care about the handwriting? I've seen him!"

"Seen him?" said Mr. Utterson. "What did you see?"

"I saw the creature," said Poole. "I came into the laboratory from the garden and it was in there looking through the boxes. It looked up when I came in, cried out and ran upstairs into the office. I saw it for only a minute, but the hair stood up on my head with fear. Sir, if that was my master, why was he wearing a mask? If it was my master, why did he cry out like a rat and run from me?"

"These are all very strange circumstances," said Mr. Utterson. "I think your master suffers from an illness that both tortures and deforms him. That explains the change in his voice and the mask and why he avoids his friends. And that is why he is so eager to find this drug."

---

□ **crumpled** 구겨진, 쭈글쭈글한
□ **compliment** 찬사, 칭찬
□ **pure** (다른 것이 섞이지 않은) 순수한, 깨끗한
□ **quantity** 양, 수량
□ **quality** 질
□ **cost** 비용, 가격
□ **urgently** 급히, 당장

□ **unquestionably** 의문의 여지가 없이, 확실하게
□ **care about** …에 관심을 가지다
□ **circumstances** 상황, 환경
□ **torture** 괴롭히다, 고문하다
□ **be eager to + 동사원형** 간절히 …하기를 원하다

1 **with the compliments of** (찬사·존경의 인사말) …로부터
To Messrs Maw, with the compliments of Dr. Jekyll.
모우 상회 귀하, 지킬 박사로부터.

"Sir," said the butler, "that thing was not my master. My master is a tall, well-built man, and this was more of a dwarf. That thing in the mask was not Dr. Jekyll. It is the belief of my heart that murder has been done."

"If that's true, it's my duty to make certain," said the lawyer. "If you believe he's been harmed, I'll have to break in that door. Who is going to help me?"

"I will, sir," said Poole bravely. "I'll take the ax from the laboratory and you take the kitchen poker."

The lawyer grasped the crude and weighty instrument in his hand.

"You know that you and I are about to place [1] ourselves in a position of some peril?" asked the lawyer.

"Yes, sir, I do," returned the butler.

"Then we should be frank with each other," said Mr. Utterson. "Did you recognize the masked figure that you saw?"

"It moved very quickly," said Poole, "but are you asking if it was Mr. Hyde? Yes, it was the same size and moved in the same way. And he could have come in by the laboratory door because when he disappeared, he still had the key. But that's not all. Have ever you met Mr. Hyde?"

"Yes," said Mr. Utterson, "I once spoke with him."

□ more of 오히려
□ dwarf 난쟁이, 왜소증 환자
□ make certain 확인하다
□ be harmed 해〔상처〕를 입다
□ break in (무리하게) 침입하다
□ ax(e) 도끼
□ kitchen poker 부지깽이

□ grasp 잡다, 쥐다
□ crude 투박한
□ weighty 무거운, 묵직한
□ instrument 도구, 기구
□ be frank with …에게 솔직하게 털어놓다
□ masked 가면을 쓴, 복면을 한

1 **place oneself in a position of** …한 상황〔처지〕에 놓이게 되다
You know that you and I are about to place ourselves in a position of some peril?
자네와 내가 곧 위험한 상황에 놓이게 되리라는 건 알고 있겠지?

"Then you know that there is something queer about
him," said Poole. "It is something that makes your
blood run cold and thin."

"Yes, I admit that I felt something of what you
describe," said Mr. Utterson.

"Well, I had that feeling when that masked thing ran
into the office," said Poole. "I know it's not evidence,
Mr. Utterson. But I give you my bible word that it was
Mr. Hyde."

"Yes," said the lawyer. "I'm afraid you might be right."

Mr. Utterson told two of the other servants to get
sticks and wait outside near the laboratory door.

"If anyone tries to come out, you must stop them,"
he said.

With the poker under his arm, the lawyer led the way
into the laboratory where they sat down to wait. From
the office, they could hear footsteps walking to and fro
along the floor.

---

□ queer 이상한, 독특한
□ give you my bible word (that)절
　성경에 손을 얹고 당신에게 …임을 맹세하다
□ lead the way into …로 앞장서다
□ to and fro 이리저리
□ lost soul 지옥에 떨어진 영혼

□ affect …에게 영향을 주다
□ demand to + 동사원형 …하는
　것을 요구하다
□ break ... down …을 부수다
□ Down with ...! …을 부수자!

"It walks up and down all day and all night," whispered Poole. "It only stops when a new sample comes from the chemist. But tell me, are those the doctor's footsteps?"

The steps fell lightly and slowly. It was very different from the heavy step of Henry Jekyll.

Mr. Utterson sighed and said, "No. Does it ever do anything else?"

Poole nodded. "I heard it weeping!"

"Weeping?" said the lawyer, with a feeling of horror.

"Weeping like a lost soul," said the butler. "It affected me so deeply in my heart that I wanted to weep, too."

Poole picked up the ax and put his candle down on a table. They went up the stairs and stopped outside the office door.

"Jekyll," shouted Mr. Utterson. "I demand to see you!"

He paused a moment, but there came no reply.

"If you do not open the door, we will break it down," he said.

"Utterson," said the voice, "for God's sake, have mercy!"

"That's not Jekyll's voice!" cried Mr. Utterson. "It's Hyde's! Down with the door, Poole!"

As Poole's ax hit the door, a scream came from
inside the office. The ax hit the door again and again
until at the fifth blow, the lock burst asunder and the
wreck of the door fell inwards on the carpet.

Mr. Utterson and Poole looked into the office. It was well lit and warm with a good fire glowing in the fireplace. Papers were neatly stacked on the desk and a tray was laid for tea near the fire. Lying face down on the floor in the middle of the room was the twitching body of a man. Mr. Utterson walked softly into the room, bent down and turned the body onto its back. It was Edward Hyde. He was dressed in clothes far too large for him and in his hand he held a small bottle.

Mr. Utterson knew that he was looking at the body of a suicide.

"We have come too late to save or punish," he said. "He is dead. Now we must find the body of your master."

They carefully examined the office and the laboratory but there was no trace of Henry Jekyll, dead or alive. Poole stamped on the flagstones of the laboratory.

☐ blow 강타, 세게 때림
☐ burst asunder 산산이 부서지다
☐ wreck 잔해, 파편
☐ inwards 안으로, 안쪽으로
☐ glow 타오르다
☐ be stacked on …에 쌓이다
☐ neatly 단정하게, 깔끔하게
☐ tray 쟁반, 받침

☐ lie face down 엎드려 누워 있다
☐ twitching 경련을 일으키는, 꿈틀거리는
☐ bend down 아래로 (몸을) 구부리다 (bend-bent-bent)
☐ suicide 자살한 사람
☐ stamp on …을 쿵쿵 밟다
☐ flagstone 판석(넓고 평평한 돌)

"Perhaps he is buried here," said Poole.

"Or he may have fled," said Mr. Utterson.

They went back up the stairs and carefully examined the contents of the office. On a table, several measured heaps of white powder lay on glass saucers. It seemed as if Hyde was preparing some experiment.

"That is the same drug that I was always bringing him," said Poole.

Next they examined the desk. A large envelope was on top of the neat pile of papers. It had Mr. Utterson's name written on it in Dr. Jekyll's handwriting. The lawyer opened it and several enclosures fell to the floor. The first document was a will. It contained the same strange clauses and conditions as the one Mr. Utterson had returned to Dr. Jekyll six months before.

But he saw with amazement that the name of Edward Hyde had been replaced with the name of Gabriel John Utterson.

### Mini-Lesson

may have p.p. : …였을지도 모른다 (약한 추측)
must have p.p. : …였음에 틀림없다 (강한 추측)

• Or he may have fled.  아니면 그는 도망쳤을지도 모르지.
• Hyde must have been enraged to see himself displaced.
  하이드는 자신이 교체된 것을 보고 격분했음에 틀림없네.

He looked at the papers, and then at the dead man
on the floor.

"My head goes around," said Mr. Utterson. "Hyde
must have been enraged to see himself displaced; yet
he has had this document in his possession for days
and has not destroyed it."

□ be buried  (땅에) 묻히다
□ flee  도망가다 (flee-fled-fled)
□ measured  계량된, 측정된
□ heap  (아무렇게나 쌓아 놓은) 더미
□ saucer  접시, 받침
□ experiment  실험
□ enclosure  (편지에) 동봉된 것

□ clause  (법적 서류의) 조항, 조목
□ one's head goes around  …의
　머리가 빙빙 돌다
□ be enraged to + 동사원형  …하고
　격분하다
□ displaced  교체된, 바뀐
□ in one's possession  …의 수중에

He picked up the next paper. It was a brief note in the doctor's handwriting and dated at the top.

"Poole!" said Mr. Utterson, "he was alive and wrote this note today. He can't have been murdered and disposed of in such a short time. He must still be alive and have fled. We must be careful. We don't want to involve your master in this catastrophe."

"Why don't you read it, sir?" asked Poole.

"I'm afraid of what he may have written," replied the lawyer, solemnly. And then he read the note:

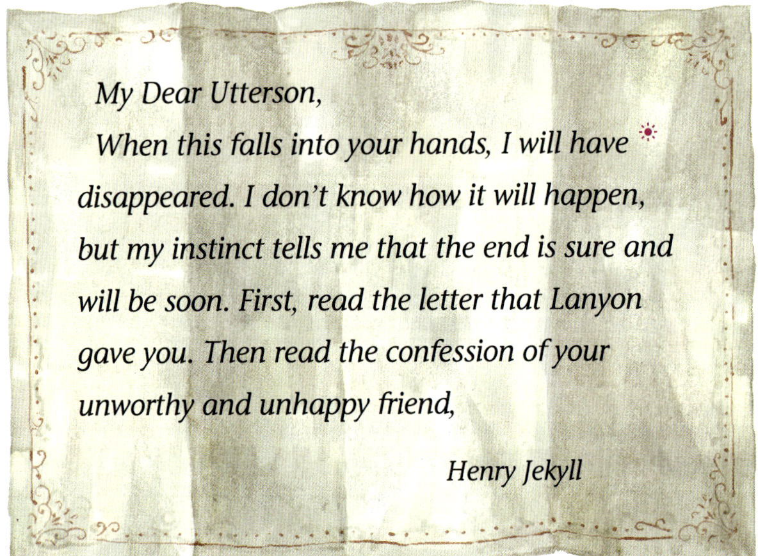

"There must be another document," said Mr. Utterson.

"Here, sir," said Poole, and gave him a large, heavy packet.

The lawyer put it in his pocket.

"Say nothing about this, Poole," he said. "It's now ten and I must go home and read these documents. I'll be back before midnight and then we will send for the police."

They went out, locking the door of the laboratory behind them. With a heavy heart, Mr. Utterson walked home to read the two letters in which this mystery would be explained.

---

☐ be dated  날짜가 적혀 있다
☐ can't have p.p.  …였을 리가 없다
☐ be disposed of  처리되다, 없애지다
☐ involve A in B  A를 B에 관련(연관)시키다
☐ catastrophe  비극, 참사

☐ fall into one's hands  …의 손에 들어가다
☐ instinct  직감, 본능
☐ confession  자백, 고백
☐ unworthy  가치 없는
☐ packet  꾸러미, 소포
☐ send for  …을 부르러 사람을 보내다

## Mini-Less🔆n

See p. 130

### 때와 조건을 나타내는 부사절의 시제

When this falls into your hands, I will have disappeared.  '이 편지가 자네 손에 들어갈 때쯤이면, 나는 종적을 감춘 상태일 걸세.'에서 when절에 현재 시제 falls를 쓴 것은 때와 조건을 나타내는 부사절에서는 미래 시제 대신 현재 시제를 쓰기 때문이랍니다.

• If you pass the audition, you will get a chance to appear on TV.
  네가 그 오디션을 통과한다면, 너는 TV에 출연할 기회를 얻게 될 거야.

# Check-up Time!

● **WORDS**

빈칸에 들어갈 알맞은 단어를 고르세요.

**1** Papers were neatly __________ on the desk.
  a. harmed          b. swept          c. stacked

**2** Poole pulled a __________ note from his pocket.
  a. crumpled          b. wholesale          c. impure

**3** Hyde must have been __________ to see himself displaced.
  a. masked          b. enraged          c. measured

● **STRUCTURE**

괄호 안의 두 단어 중 알맞은 것에 동그라미 하세요.

**1** He is shut up (on / in) his study.

**2** We should be frank (with / of) each other.

**3** Mr. Utterson bent (up / down) and turned the body onto its back.

**4** He can't have been disposed (of / off) in such a short time.

**5** It doesn't commend itself (of / to) reason.

● **COMPREHENSION**

본문의 내용과 일치하면 T에, 일치하지 않으면 F에 표시하세요.

T   F

**1** Mr. Utterson received a note from Dr. Jekyll asking for money. ☐ ☐

**2** Poole went to the chemist and brought back the drug. ☐ ☐

**3** Mr. Utterson saw Mr. Hyde running away from him. ☐ ☐

**4** Poole entered Dr. Jekyll's office by using an ax. ☐ ☐

● **SUMMARY**

빈칸에 맞는 말을 골라 이야기를 완성하세요.

One evening, Poole came to Mr. Utterson and told that Dr. Jekyll might have been (   ). Mr. Utterson was so surprised that he went to Dr. Jekyll's house with Poole. Mr. Utterson and Poole (   ) down the door to Dr. Jekyll's office and found Mr. Hyde lying dead and a large (   ) on the desk. It contained Dr. Jekyll's will and a brief (   ) in the doctor's handwriting for Mr. Utterson.

a. note    b. murdered    c. envelope    d. broke

# CHAPTER 6

# Dr. Lanyon's Letter
래니언박사의편지

Mr. Utterson entered his office and locked the door. Then he sat at his desk and opened the envelope he had received on the day of Dr. Lanyon's funeral. He began to read.

Four days ago, on the evening of the ninth of January, an envelope addressed in the handwriting of Doctor Henry Jekyll was delivered to me. I was greatly surprised because we are not in the habit of correspondence and I had dined with him the night before. The contents increased my wonder. This is what Dr. Jekyll had written:

*Dear Lanyon,*

*You are one of my oldest friends and although we may have differed at times on scientific questions, I cannot remember any break in our friendship. Tonight, my life, my reputation and my sanity are in your hands. If you fail me, I am destroyed.*

*Please postpone all other arrangements for tonight. Take a cab and bring this letter with you to my house.*

*Poole, my butler, will be waiting for you with a locksmith. Have the locksmith open the door of my office. Go in alone and open the cupboard, labeled E, on the left side. The fourth drawer from the top contains some paper-wrapped powders, a small glass bottle, and a memorandum book.*

*Please take this drawer and its contents back to your house.*

□ be delivered to ⋯에게 배달되다
□ be in the habit of ⋯의 습관이 있다
□ correspondence 서신 교환
□ dine with ⋯와 식사를 하다
□ differ on ⋯에 대해 의견이 다르다
□ break in ⋯의 중단〔균열〕
□ reputation 명성, 명예
□ sanity 온전한 정신
□ fail ⋯에게 도움이 되지 못하다

□ be destroyed 죽게 되다
□ postpone 미루다, 연기하다
□ arrangement 일정, 예정
□ cab 마차
□ locksmith 자물쇠 수리공
□ labeled ⋯라고 표시가 된
□ paper-wrapped 종이로 싸여진
□ memorandum book 비망록

*At midnight, please be alone in your consulting room.*
*A man will come to see you. Give him the drawer. If you insist*
*on an explanation, you will have it five minutes later.*
*I know you will not let me down. Think of me now, in a* [1]
*strange place and in great distress. If you do as I ask, my*
*troubles will rapidly leave me. Help me, my dear Lanyon.*

*Your friend,*

*H. Jekyll*


*P.S. If this letter does not arrive until tomorrow morning,*
*please do my errand as soon as you can. And then expect*
*my messenger at midnight tomorrow. If that night passes*
*without a visit from my messenger, you will have seen the*
*last of Henry Jekyll.*


After reading this letter, I was sure Jekyll was insane
but until that was proved beyond all doubt, I felt bound [2]
to do as he requested. I found a cab and went straight
to his house. The butler was waiting for me with a
locksmith. As instructed, I took out the drawer from
the cupboard, tied it in a sheet and returned home.

□ consulting room 진찰실
□ insist on …을 주장〔고집〕하다
□ in distress 괴로운, 고통스러운
□ do one's errand …의 부탁을
　들어주다

□ insane 정신 이상의, 미친
□ beyond all doubt 모든 의심을
　뒤로하고
□ tie ... in a sheet …을 종이에
　싸서 묶다

**1　let ... down** …을 실망시키다
I know you will not let me down.
나는 자네가 나를 실망시키지 않을 것임을 알고 있네.

**2　feel bound to + 동사원형** …해야 한다는 생각이 들다
I felt bound to do as he requested.
나는 그가 요구한 대로 해야 한다는 생각이 들었다네.

In my consulting room, I proceeded to examine its contents. The wrappers contained what seemed to be a common white salt. The bottle was half-full of blood-red liquid with a strong smell of phosphorus and ether. The book contained a series of dated entries covering a period of many years, but these stopped about a year ago. I assumed the book was a record of some unsuccessful experiments.

1 **could just as well have + p.p.**  …하는 것도 괜찮을 뻔했다
His messenger could just as well have followed his instructions.
그의 심부름꾼이 그의 지시들을 따르는 것도 괜찮을 뻔했는데.

There was nothing to suggest why Jekyll had involved me in this. His messenger could just as well [1] have followed his instructions. And why was this messenger to be received by me in secret? The more I reflected, the more convinced I grew that I was dealing with a case of brain disease.

**(?)** Which is not the contents of the drawer?
a. white salt
b. blood-red liquid
c. memorandum book

정답은 c

□ proceed to + 동사원형  계속해서 …하다
□ wrapper  포장지
□ common  평범한, 일반적인
□ half-full of  …로 반쯤 찬
□ blood-red  피처럼 붉은
□ phosphorus  인(비금속 원소)
□ ether  에테르(마취제로 쓰이는 알코올 추출물)

□ dated  날짜가 적혀진
□ entry  (사전이나 일기 등의) 항목
□ assume (that)절  …일 것이라고 가정하다(추측하다)
□ unsuccessful  성공하지 못한
□ reflect  깊이(곰곰이) 생각하다
□ convinced  확신하는
□ deal with  …을 다루다
□ brain disease  정신병, 뇌 질환

## Mini-Less☀n

**the + 비교급(A), the + 비교급(B)**  See p. 131

'A하면 할수록, 더 B하다'라는 표현은 「the + 비교급(A), the + 비교급(B)」로 나타낸답니다.

• The more I reflected, the more convinced I grew that I was dealing with a case of brain disease.  생각하면 할수록, 내가 정신병자의 사건을 다루고 있다는 확신이 더 들었네.
• The sooner it gets dark, the sooner he will come back.
빨리 어두워지면 질수록, 그가 더 빨리 돌아올 텐데.

At twelve o'clock, I heard a knock on the door.
I opened it and found a small man crouching against
the pillars of the porch. I invited him inside. The
room was brightly lit and I had a chance to clearly
see him. He was small and muscular with a most
unpleasant expression on his face. I felt an immediate
dislike for him even though he seemed to be weak
and ill.

His clothes, although they were of good, expensive [1]
fabric, were enormously large for him. The trousers
were rolled up to keep them from dragging on the [2]
ground and the waist of the coat hung to his
buttocks. The collar of the coat was almost as wide as
his shoulders. But I did not feel the urge to laugh at
him. There was something abnormal and revolting
about him.

□ pillar 기둥
□ porch 현관
□ muscular 근육질의
□ fabric 옷감, 천
□ enormously 엄청나게, 무척
□ trousers 바지
□ be rolled up 말아 올려져 있다
□ drag (바닥에) 끌리다
□ hang to …에 들러붙다

□ buttocks 엉덩이
□ feel the urge to＋동사원형 …하고
　싶은 충동을 느끼다
□ abnormal 비정상적인
□ revolting 혐오스러운, 역겨운
□ shake ... off …을 떨쳐내다
□ be seated 앉다, 착석하다
□ lose the battle with …와의
　싸움에서 지다

"Have you got it?" cried the man.

He was so impatient that he even put his hand on my arm. I felt cold at his touch and shook him off.

"Come, sir," I said. "Be seated, if you please."

"I beg your pardon, Dr. Lanyon," he replied. "My patience has lost the battle with my politeness. I came here on important business at the request of [3] Dr. Henry Jekyll. I believe you have something to give me."

? Which is not true about Mr. Hyde?

   a. He was wearing good and expensive clothes.
   b. His trousers were dragging on the ground.
   c. The collar of his coat was as wide as his shoulders.

---

1 **of** (재료) …로 만든(된)

His clothes, although they were of good, expensive fabric, were enormously large for him.
그의 옷은 좋고 비싼 옷감으로 만든 것이었지만 그에게 무척이나 컸다네.

2 **keep + 명사(A) + from + …ing(B)** A가 B하지 않도록 하다

The trousers were rolled up to keep them from dragging on the ground.
바지가 바닥에 끌리지 않도록 하기 위해 말아 올려져 있었다네.

3 **at the request of** …의 요청으로

I came here on important business at the request of Dr. Henry Jekyll. 저는 헨리 지킬 박사님의 요청으로 중요한 임무를 띠고 여기에 왔습니다.

"There it is, sir," I said, pointing to the drawer that lay on the floor covered with a sheet.

He laid his hand over his heart as if he were in pain. [1] Then he went to the drawer and pulled away the sheet. At the sight of its contents, he uttered one loud sob of such immense relief that I was petrified.

"Do you have a measuring glass?" he asked.

I found a glass and he measured out a small quantity of the red mixture and added one of the powders. The mixture began to brighten in color as the powder dissolved. Then it began to bubble and give off a vapor. Suddenly, it stopped bubbling and changed to a dark purple. Then it slowly faded to a pale green. My visitor smiled and put the glass on the desk.

"And now," he said, "to settle what remains. If you ask me to take this glass and leave your house, your life will not change. But if you allow me to stay, new knowledge and the possibility of fame will be yours. You will see a miracle to rival the powers of God or Satan."

---

1 **as if + 주어 + were / 과거형 동사** 마치 …인 것처럼
He laid his hand over his heart as if he were in pain.
그는 마치 고통스러운 것처럼 손을 심장에 갖다대었네.

- pull away ···을 떼다
- utter (소리나 말 등)을 입 밖으로 내다
- sob 흐느낌
- immense 엄청난, 어마어마한
- be petrified 겁에 질리다
- measuring glass (눈금이 있는) 계량컵, 시험관
- measure out ···을 덜어내다
- mixture 혼합물
- dissolve 녹다, 용해되다
- bubble 거품이 생기다
- give off (기체나 냄새 등)을 내다 〔발산하다〕
- vapor 수증기, 증기
- fade to ···로 연해〔옅어〕지다
- settle 해결하다
- possibility 가능성
- fame 명예, 명성
- rival ···에 필적하다〔비할 만하다〕
- Satan 사탄, 악마

"Sir," I said, calmly, "you speak enigmatically, and I have never believed in miracles. But I have done an inexplicable service for a friend and cannot stop now before I see the end."

"Then what follows must remain bound by the [1] secrecy of our profession," said the man. "You have always had narrow views, but watch this miracle!"

He put the glass to his lips and drank the contents at one gulp. He cried out and then he staggered and clutched the table. He held on, gasping with an open mouth and staring eyes. And as I looked, he seemed to swell. His face turned black and the features seemed to melt and alter. I pressed myself against the wall and raised my arm to protect myself from the creature.

---

□ enigmatically 수수께끼 같이, 알쏭달쏭하게
□ do a ... service ···한 부탁을 들어주다
□ inexplicable 설명이 안 되는, 불가해한
□ secrecy 비밀 유지, 비밀인 상태
□ profession 직업
□ at one gulp 단숨에, 한입에

□ stagger 비틀거리다
□ clutch 꽉 쥐다
□ hold on 계속 붙잡고 있다
□ gasp 헐떡거리다
□ swell 부풀어 오르다
□ melt 녹아내리다
□ press A against B A를 B에 기대다
□ protect A from B A를 B로부터 보호하다(지키다)

---

1  **remain bound by** ···로 속박되다(묶이다)
What follows must remain bound by the secrecy of our profession.
이 다음에 일어나는 일은 직업상의 비밀로 속박되는 것입니다.

"Oh God! Oh God!" I screamed again and again.

Henry Jekyll stood before me. He was pale, shaken and half fainting like a man brought back from death. He had changed from one thing to another in front of my eyes!

What he told me in the next hour I cannot bring my mind to set on paper. I saw what I saw and my soul sickened at it. My life is shaken to its roots and sleep [1] has left me. The deadliest terror is with me at all hours of the day and night. I feel that my days are numbered, and I will die refusing to believe the horrifying thing that I saw.

Jekyll confessed that the creature that crept to my house that night was known by the name of Hyde. You will have heard by now that he is the murderer [2] of Sir Danvers Carew.

Your friend,

Hastie Lanyon

---

□ shaken 겁먹은, 충격을 받은
□ half fainting 반쯤 기절한
□ brought back from death 죽었다 깨어난
□ bring one's mind …을 기억하다
□ set ... on paper …을 글로 옮기다
□ sicken at …로 인해 병들다

□ at all hours 시도 때도 없이
□ one's days are numbered 살날이 얼마 남지 않다
□ die ...ing …하면서 죽다
□ creep to …로 몰래 들어가다 (creep - crept - crept)
□ by now 지금쯤이면

1 **be shaken to one's roots** 뿌리째 흔들리다
My life is shaken to its roots and sleep has left me.
내 인생이 뿌리째 흔들려 있고 한숨도 잘 수 없다네.

2 **will + have + p.p.** …할 것이다 (미래완료)
You will have heard by now that he is the murderer of Sir Danvers Carew.
자네도 지금쯤이면 그가 댄버스 캐류 경의 살인범이라는 것을 들었을 것이네.

# Check-up Time!

● **WORDS**

빈칸에 알맞은 단어를 보기에서 골라 써넣으세요.

| secrecy | vapor | fabric | gulp |
|---|---|---|---|

**1** He drank the contents at one __________.

**2** It began to bubble and give off a __________.

**3** His clothes were of good and expensive __________.

**4** What follows must remain bound by the __________ of our profession.


● **STRUCTURE**

괄호 안에 알맞은 것을 골라 문장을 완성하세요.

**1** He laid his hand over his heart as if he (is / were) in pain.

**2** The trousers were rolled up to keep them (to / from) dragging on the ground.

**3** In my consulting room, I proceeded (to examine / examining) its contents.

Words | 1. gulp  2. vapor  3. fabric  4. secrecy
Structure | 1. were  2. from  3. to examine

다음은 누가 한 말일까요? 기호를 써넣으세요.

a.

Mr. Hyde

b.

Dr. Lanyon

**1** "Do you have a measuring glass?" _______

**2** "Be seated, if you please." _______

**3** "You have always had narrow views." _______

● SUMMARY

빈칸에 맞는 말을 골라 이야기를 완성하세요.

After the (　　) of Dr. Lanyon, Mr. Utterson read the letter from him. It said that he received a letter from Dr. Jekyll and followed his (　　). Dr. Lanyon went to Dr. Jekyll's house and returned home with the (　　). At midnight, a small and unpleasant man arrived and demanded to see it. He mixed the (　　) of the drawer and swallowed the mixture. After he drank all of it, he changed to Dr. Jekyll.

a. contents

b. drawer

c. funeral

d. instructions

ANSWERS

# CHAPTER 7

# Dr. Jekyll's Story

지킬 박사의 이야기

Mr. Utterson put Dr. Lanyon's letter aside and shook his head in disbelief. Then he opened the package he had found in Henry Jekyll's office. He unfolded the papers and began to read.

I was born into a wealthy family with a large fortune. I grew to be handsome, diligent and ambitious. I became a doctor and was well respected by my colleagues and friends. I had, however, a wild side to my nature. I became addicted to drugs and alcohol and lusted after the pleasures of the flesh.

□ put ... aside ···을 옆으로 치우다
□ in disbelief 믿기지 않는다는 듯이
□ unfold 펼치다
□ be born into a ... family ···한 집안에 태어나다
□ fortune 부(富), 재산
□ nature 본성
□ become addicted to ···에 중독되다

□ lust after ···을 열망〔갈망〕하다
□ flesh 육체, 살
□ wicked 못된, 사악한
□ curse 저주
□ mankind 인류
□ daydream about ···에 대해 공상을 하다
□ separate 분리하다

1 **struggle to + 동사원형** ···하려고 애쓰다〔노력하다〕
I struggled to control myself. 나는 내 자신을 통제하려고 애썼네.

I struggled to control myself and sometimes failed, [1] but for many years I successfully hid this side of my nature. And I did so with a terrible sense of shame.

I knew that many men enjoyed these pleasures but my high hopes for my future made my wicked pleasures seem much worse. I began to think about the constant battle all men fight between good and evil and concluded that every man has two real but different sides to his nature. And it was the curse of mankind that these twin natures constantly struggled within one man. I daydreamed about the possibility of separating these two natures and began to experiment.

### Mini-Lesson

**결과를 나타내는 to 부정사**

I grew to be handsome, diligent and ambitious. '나는 자라서 잘생기고 근면하며 야심차게 되었네.'에서 to be는 동사 grew에 이은 결과를 나타내어 '…해서 ~되다(하다)'로 해석하면 돼요.

- He returned from work to find his wife gone.
  그는 직장에서 돌아와서 아내가 사라졌다는 것을 알았다.

Eventually I invented a drug that I believed would remove the moral side of my nature whenever I chose, allowing my darker side to emerge.

I hesitated for a long time before I used the drug but in the end the temptation was too great. Late one night, I mixed the elements and watched them boil and smoke together in the glass. When the bubbling stopped, I drank the life-changing liquid.

I immediately felt terrible pains, a grinding in my bones, and dreadful sickness. I can't describe the feeling of horror deep within my soul. Then these pains began to disappear and I felt physically younger and fitter with a freedom of the soul previously unknown to me. I knew immediately that this new personality would be ten times stronger than my  original evil side. The thought delighted me. I stretched out my hands and saw that I had physically changed, too. I was much shorter than before with bony, hairy hands!

□ moral 도덕적인; 도덕심
□ emerge (어둠이나 숨어 있던 곳에서) 나오다, 모습을 드러내다
□ in the end 결국, 마침내
□ temptation 유혹
□ boil 끓다
□ life-changing 인생을 바꿔놓을
□ grinding 분쇄

□ physically 신체〔육체〕적으로
□ fit 건강한
□ personality 인격, 성격
□ stretch out one's hands …의 손을 펴다
□ bony 뼈가 앙상한
□ hairy 털이 많은

## Mini-Lesson

### 배수 + 형용사의 비교급 + than

two〔three, four …〕times와 같은 배수 다음에 「형용사의 비교급 + than」이 오면 '…배는 더 ~한'을 뜻하는 표현이 만들어진답니다.

- I knew immediately that this new personality would be ten times stronger than my original evil side.
  나는 즉시 이 새로운 인격이 원래 나의 사악한 면보다 열 배는 더 강하리라는 것을 알았네.
- This book is three times thicker than yours. 이 책은 네 책보다 세 배는 더 두껍다.

There was no mirror in my office but I had to see the changes. I tiptoed through the house to the mirror in my room and saw Edward Hyde for the first time. I saw that he was much smaller, slighter and younger than Henry Jekyll. The evil showed plainly on his face and gave an impression of deformity but to me it seemed natural and human. I still had to complete my experiment. I did not know yet if I had lost my good side forever. I went back to the office, prepared more of the drug and drank it down. After more terrible pain and suffering, I regained the character, body and face of Henry Jekyll.

The next day, I rented an apartment in Soho and opened a bank account in the name of Edward Hyde. I told my servants that Mr. Hyde would sometimes be seen in the house and that they were to treat him with respect.

---

□ tiptoe 까치발을 하고 살금살금 걷다
□ slight 가냘픈, 작고 여윈
□ plainly 명백히
□ give an impression of …의 인상
　을 주다
□ complete 완성하다, 끝내다
□ suffering 고통
□ regain 되찾다, 회복하다

□ forbidden 금지된
□ sordid 비도덕적인, 추악한
□ undignified 품위 없는, 채신 없는
□ monstrous 흉포한, 괴물 같은
□ behavior 행동
□ awake (잠에서) 깨다
　(awake - awoke - awoken)
□ sensation 느낌, 감각

The forbidden pleasures that I had enjoyed as Jekyll
were sordid and undignified, but in the hands of
Edward Hyde, they became monstrous. Jekyll was
often shocked by the behavior of Hyde, but he had no
power to stop him.

About two months before the murder of Sir Danvers,
I returned home at a late hour and awoke the next
morning with some strange sensations. I looked down
and saw that my hand was the hand of Edward Hyde!

I rushed to the mirror and my blood froze with fear.
I had gone to bed as Henry Jekyll and I had awoken as
Edward Hyde. For a moment, I panicked. Then I
dressed and went to my office. Ten minutes later,
Dr. Jekyll had returned to his own shape and was [1]
sitting down to breakfast.

I began to think more seriously about the problems
of my double life. The part of me that was Hyde was
being used more often and growing stronger. It was
becoming more difficult to hold onto my better self.
I knew this could be dangerous. If the evil side of my
nature took complete control, the character of Edward [2]
Hyde would become permanent.

□ **rush to** …로 급하게 가다
□ **freeze with fear** 공포로 얼어붙다
  (freeze – froze – frozen)
□ **panic** 겁(공포)에 질리다, 공황
  상태에 빠지다
  (panic – panicked – panicked)
□ **sit down to breakfast** 아침 식사
  자리에 앉다
□ **double life** 이중생활

□ **hold onto** …을 지키다(고수하다)
□ **complete** 완전한, 완벽한
□ **character** 성격, 특징
□ **permanent** 영구적인, 영원한
□ **give up** 포기하다, 처분하다
□ **be tortured with** …로 고통을 받다
□ **longing** 갈망, 열망
□ **compound** 혼합하다, 제조하다
□ **swallow** 삼키다

1 **return to one's own shape** …의 본모습으로 되돌아오다
  Ten minutes later, Dr. Jekyll had returned to his own shape.
  10분 후에, 지킬 박사는 그의 본모습으로 되돌아왔네.

The good Henry Jekyll would disappear forever.
I knew I must choose between these two and in the
end chose to keep the better part of my nature. But
I did not give up the house in Soho or destroy Hyde's
clothes. Perhaps I knew this choice wouldn't last.

For two months, however, I led a more moral life
than I had ever done
before. But after a while, I
was once more tortured
with longings. Hyde was
struggling for freedom.
At last, in a moment
of moral weakness,
I compounded and
swallowed the
drug.

2 **take control** 장악하다, 통제하다
If the evil side of my nature took complete control, the character
of Edward Hyde would become permanent.
만약 내 본성의 악한 면이 완전히 장악한다면, 에드워드 하이드의 성격은 영구적이 될 것이네.

I had never really thought about the true character
of Edward Hyde. I knew he lacked morals but I did
not understand that he was absolutely evil. I soon
discovered this. Hyde had been controlled for too long
and he came out roaring mad and ready to do his worst.
I don't know what made me attack Sir Danvers, but as
I beat and kicked his poor old body I delighted in every
blow. My lust for evil was satisfied for the moment.

I ran to the house in Soho and destroyed my papers.
Then I hurried back to the laboratory. Hyde thought
about his crime with pleasure and sang as he mixed the
drug. But before the pain of change had disappeared,
Henry Jekyll was begging forgiveness from God. I cried
and prayed and tried to drown out the ugly images in
my head. And then I saw the solution to the problem.
Hyde must disappear forever. I locked the laboratory
door that Hyde had so often used, and broke the key.

1 **relieve one's suffering**  …의 고통을 줄여주다
   You know how hard I worked last year to help others and
   relieve their suffering.  내가 지난 해에 얼마나 열심히 다른 사람들을 돕고 그들의
   고통을 줄여주기 위해 애썼는지 자네도 알고 있지 않나.

2 **be tempted to + 동사원형**  …하고 싶은 유혹을 느끼다
   I was tempted to become the secret sinner.
   나는 비밀스러운 죄인이 되고 싶은 유혹을 느꼈네.

The next day came the news that someone had witnessed the murder. Hyde's guilt was known to the world. If I let him escape for an instant, he would be caught and hanged for the crime and I would be dead too. Only the character of Jekyll could keep him safe. I had to make Hyde disappear forever.

You know how hard I worked last year to help others and relieve their suffering. The days passed quietly [1] and almost happily but I had not lost my wicked side. I was tempted to become the secret sinner that I had [2] been in my youth, but I never dreamed of releasing Hyde again.

(?) Henry Jekyll locked the laboratory door
└ and broke the ____________ .

정답 key

□ lack ···이 부족하다〔없다〕
□ absolutely 절대적으로
□ roaring mad 미쳐서 으르렁거리는
   〔아우성치는〕
□ delight 기쁨을 느끼다
□ in every blow 칠 때마다
□ lust for ···을 향한 갈망〔욕망〕
□ be satisfied 만족되다, 충족되다
□ beg forgiveness from ···에게
   용서를 구하다

□ drown out 몰아내다
□ solution to ···에 대한 해결책
□ guilt 죄
□ be known to the world 세상에
   알려지다
□ for an instant 잠깐 동안, 일순간
□ be hanged for ···로 교수형을 당하다
□ keep ... safe ···을 안전하게 지키다
□ sinner 죄인
□ dream of ...ing ···하는 상상을 하다

One day, I sat in the sun on a bench in Regent's Park. It was a fine, clear January day. The evil beast within me stirred but my good side was not yet moved to begin. I thought about the good things I had done and would do in the future. And at that moment, a horrible sickness and trembling came over me. Then I began to feel a strong excitement and energy. I saw that my clothes hung on my body and the hand that lay on my knee was bony and hairy. I was once more Edward Hyde. I was a hunted, homeless murderer.

My drugs were in one of the cupboards of my office,
but how could I reach them? I thought of Lanyon and
I knew what I must do. I found a cab and drove to
a hotel in Portland. I took a private room and wrote
a note to Lanyon and one to Poole. Then I asked the
hotel porter to have them hand-delivered.

After that, I, as Hyde, sat all day by the fire in the
hotel room. When darkness came, I went to Lanyon's
house, counting the minutes until midnight.

When I took the drug at Lanyon's, my old friend's
horror deeply affected me. I no longer feared hanging
for the terrible murder of Sir Danvers. It was the horror [1]
of being Hyde that frightened me. I came home and got
into bed. When I awoke in the morning, I was weak but
refreshed and still myself.

☐ stir 꿈틀거리다, 움직이기 시작하다
☐ be moved to + 동사원형 …할 마음이
　 들다
☐ come over …을 덮치다
☐ hunted 쫓기는
☐ homeless 집이 없는, 노숙자의

☐ porter 짐꾼
☐ hand-delivered 인편으로 전달되는
☐ no longer 더 이상 …않다
☐ hang for …로 교수형을 당하다
☐ get into bed 잠자리에 들다
☐ refreshed 기분이 상쾌한

1 **It was + 강조할 어구(A) + that절(B)** B한 것은 바로 A였다
  It was the horror of being Hyde that frightened me.
  나를 두렵게 한 것은 바로 하이드가 된다는 공포였네.

I was in the courtyard after breakfast that morning
when I was overcome with sickness and trembling.
I barely had time to reach my office before I was Hyde
once again. It took a double dose to bring me back.
These changes began to happen more frequently. If
I slept or even relaxed for a moment, I became Hyde.
I grew weaker and Hyde's power seemed to grow
stronger. But Hyde feared my power to cut him off by
suicide, and I began to pity him.

You will learn from Poole how he searched London
for the drugs I needed. None were ever found. I now
believe that my original supply of powders was
impure, and that is why the mixture worked.

□ be overcome with …에 사로잡히다
□ barely 간신히 …하다
□ dose (약의) 1회 복용량, 투여량
□ frequently 자주, 빈번하게
□ cut ... off by suicide 자살로
　　…의 목숨을 끊다
□ pity 동정하다, 불쌍히 여기다
□ supply 준비품, 공급품
□ statement 진술서

□ under the influence of …의 영향
아래에서
□ think one's own thoughts
스스로 생각하다
□ tear ... to pieces …을 갈기갈기
찢다
□ lay down …을 내려놓다
(lay - laid - laid)

1　**bring the life of ... to an end** …의 삶을 끝내다
I bring the life of the unhappy Henry Jekyll to an end.
나는 불행한 헨리 지킬의 삶을 끝내는 것이네.

I am finishing this statement under the influence of the last of the old drugs. This is the last time that I will think my own thoughts or see my own face in the mirror. I must hurry to finish this confession. If the change takes place while I am writing it, Hyde will tear it to pieces.

As I lay down my pen and seal my confession, I bring the life of the [1] unhappy Henry Jekyll to an end. Because no [2] matter how long Hyde might live after the next change takes place, this is the true moment of my death.

2  **no matter how long + 주어(A) + 동사(B)** 얼마나 오래 A가 B하든지
No matter how long Hyde might live after the next change takes place, this is the true moment of my death.
다음 번 변화가 일어난 후에 얼마나 오래 하이드가 살든지, 지금이 진정 내가 죽는 순간이네.

# Check-up Time!

## ● WORDS

단어와 단어의 뜻을 서로 연결하세요.

1  emerge       •        • a.  evil or sinful

2  regain       •        • b.  to mix or combine ingredients

3  slight       •        • c.  to get it back again what you
                               have lost

4  wicked       •        • d.  slender or slim

5  compound  •           • e.  to come out of a dark or
                               hidden place

## ● STRUCTURE

괄호 안의 두 단어 중 알맞은 것에 동그라미 하세요.

1  I lusted (from / after) the pleasures of the flesh.

2  I became addicted (to / at) drugs and alcohol.

3  He would be caught and hanged (of / for) the crime.

4  I rushed to the mirror and my blood froze (from / with) fear.

5  At that moment, a horrible sickness and trembling came
   (above / over) me.

빈칸에 알맞은 내용을 찾아 문장을 완성하세요.

**1** When Dr. Jekyll saw Hyde in the mirror, he looked ________.

 a. much older and taller than Jekyll

 b. much smaller and slighter than Jekyll

**2** Dr. Jekyll went to ________ house and took his drug.

 a. Dr. Lanyon's

 b. Mr. Utterson's

● SUMMARY

빈칸에 맞는 말을 골라 이야기를 완성하세요.

Dr. Jekyll left a final letter for Mr. Utterson. He was born into a (　) family, but he began to think about good and evil, two different sides to human nature. So he invented a drug to (　) these two natures. When he took the drug, he changed physically and his evil side grew stronger. He began to enjoy the (　) pleasures. But his wicked side became so strong that he couldn't control it, so he finally decided to (　) his life.

a. wealthy　　b. forbidden　　c. end　　d. separate

ANSWERS

Comprehension | 1. b　2. a　　Summary | a, d, b, c

# After the Story

# He had disappeared as if he had never existed.

그는 마치 원래 존재하지 않았던 것처럼 사라져 버렸다.

★ ★ ★

댄버스 경 살인 사건의 범인으로 지목된 하이드 씨를 잡기 위해 수천 파운드의 현상금이 걸리지만 그는 위의 문장과 같이 마치 원래 존재하지 않았던 것처럼 사라져 버리는데요, 이처럼 as if 다음에 가정법 과거완료, 즉 had + p.p.가 오면 주절보다 더 전에 일어난 사실을 가정하는 표현이 만들어져 '마치 …했던 것처럼'이라는 뜻이 된답니다. 그럼 엔필드 씨와 어터슨 씨의 대화로 다시 살펴볼까요?

I disliked Mr. Hyde as if he had done something terrible to me.

그가 나에게 무슨 끔찍한 짓을 저지른 것처럼 나는 하이드 씨가 싫었어요.

Mr. Enfield

I can totally understand your feelings because I felt the same way.

자네의 기분을 충분히 이해할 수 있다네. 왜냐하면 나도 똑같이 느꼈거든.

Mr. Utterson

# Only when they had left the street far behind them did Mr. Utterson speak.

그들이 그 거리에서 한참 멀어지고 나서야 어터슨 씨는 입을 열었다.

★　★　★

산책을 즐기던 어터슨 씨와 엔필드 씨는 자신의 집 2층 창문에 있는 밝은 얼굴의 지킬 박사를 보게 됩니다. 하지만 그의 표정은 한 순간에 공포와 절망으로 바뀌고, 이 모습에 놀라 어터슨 씨는 거리에서 한참 멀어지고 난 후에야 입을 여는데요, 위 문장에서 only + 부사(절)를 강조하기 위해 문두에 두었기 때문에 그 뒤는 어순이 도치되어 do동사/조동사 + 주어 + 동사원형이 되었답니다. 뉴컴 경감과 하녀의 대화로 살펴볼까요?

Inspector
Newcomen

I heard that you fainted when you saw
Mr. Hyde killing Sir Danvers.

하이드 씨가 댄버스 경을 살해하는 장면을 보고 기절했다고
들었습니다.

Maid

Yes, it was so horrible. Only after three hours
did I come to myself.

네, 정말 끔찍했어요. 세 시간이 지난 다음에야 저는 정신을
차렸어요.

# When this falls into your hands, I will have disappeared.

이 편지가 자네 손에 들어갈 때쯤이면, 나는 종적을 감춘 후일 걸세.

★　★　★

지킬 박사가 살해당했을지도 모른다는 집사 풀의 말에 어터슨 씨는 박사의 방에 들어가는데요, 그곳에서 어터슨 씨는 위와 같은 내용의 편지 한 통을 발견합니다. 여기에서 **when**절에 미래 시제(**will fall**)가 아닌 현재 시제(**falls**)를 쓴 것은 때와 조건을 나타내는 부사절에서는 미래 시제 대신 현재 시제를 쓰기 때문이랍니다. 풀과 지킬 박사의 대화로 살펴볼까요?

Poole

How long are you going to continue your experiment, Dr. Jekyll?

지킬 박사님, 얼마나 오랫동안 실험을 계속하실 생각이신가요?

Dr. Jekyll

I will have completed my experiment when I invent a drug that will remove the moral side of me.

나의 도덕적인 면을 제거할 수 있는 약을 발명하게 되면 실험이 완료될 것이네.

The more I reflected, the more convinced I grew that I was dealing with a case of brain disease.

생각하면 할수록, 내가 정신병자의 사건을 다루고 있다는 확신이 더 들었네.

★　★　★

래니언 박사는 어터슨 씨에게 남긴 편지에서 지킬 박사의 사건에 대해 생각하면 할수록 지킬 박사의 정신 상태가 정상이 아니라는 확신이 든다는 말을 남기는데요, 이를 나타내는 위 문장은 'A하면 할수록, 더 B하다' 라는 뜻의 the + 비교급(A), the + 비교급(B)을 써서 나타냈답니다. 그럼 래니언 박사와 어터슨 씨의 대화로 살펴볼까요?

Dr. Lanyon

The more I came to know about Dr. Jekyll, the more I became suspicious that his mind went wrong.

지킬 박사에 대해서 알게 되면 될수록, 그의 정신이 이상해졌다는 의심이 더 들었네.

Mr. Utterson

I am really sorry to hear that from you.

자네에게 그런 이야기를 듣다니 무척 유감이군.

# 01 동일한 자음은 한 번만!

같은 자음은 물론, 비슷한 자음도 한 번만 발음해 주세요.

동일한 자음이 중복되면 그 발음은 한 번만 해야 한다는 사실, 알고 계시죠? 그런데 비슷한 자음이 연속해서 나올 경우에도 앞의 자음은 발음하지 않고 뒤의 자음으로 한 번만 발음한답니다. 그럼 이렇게 중복되는 자음의 발음을 본문 20쪽에서 살펴볼까요?

He ( ① ) that door, took out a key and disappeared inside.

① **went to** [웬트 투]가 아니라 [웬 투]로 자음 t를 한 번만 발음해 보세요.

He ( ② ) stay with us until morning and cash the check himself.

② **offered to** [오퍼드 투]가 아닌 앞의 자음 d를 생략하고 뒤의 자음 t만 발음해 [오퍼 투]라고 발음해 보세요.

# t와 d가 반모음과 만났을 때~

t나 d 뒤에 반모음이 오면 [t+j]는 [tʃ], [d+j]는 [dʒ]로 발음해야 해요.

signature나 could you와 같이 한 단어나 단어와 단어 사이에서 t나 d 뒤에 반모음이 오면 [t+j]는 [tʃ], [d+j]는 [dʒ]로 바뀌어서 소리가 난답니다. 그러니까 [시그니텨]가 아닌 [시그니쳐], [쿠드 유]가 아닌 [쿠 쥬]로 발음된다는 거죠. 이처럼 자음과 반모음이 만나 다른 음으로 소리 나는 단어들을 본문 26쪽과 29쪽에서 확인해 볼까요?

Mr. Utterson thought the conditions of inheritance, although not unlawful, were ( ① ) and immoral.

① **unnatural** [언내튜럴]이 아닌 [언내츄럴]로 발음해 주세요.

"( ② ) ever come across a friend of his called Hyde?"

② **Did you** [디드 유]라구요? 아니죠, [디 쥬]로 바꿔서 발음해 주면 된답니다.

## 03 발음의 고수만이 할 수 있는 r과 l

world의 r과 l은 모두 발음해 주세요.

world의 정확한 발음을 알고 있나요? r 다음에 l을 이어서 발음해야 하는 경우에는 약해지거나 생략되는 자음 없이 두 자음 모두 제대로 발음해야 해요. 우선 혀를 구부려 [워r]라고 발음한 다음 혀끝을 윗니 뒤에 붙였다가 떼면서 [을ㄷ]를 연결하면 된답니다. 따라서 [워r을ㄷ]가 되죠. 그럼 다음의 예를 본문 40쪽에서 살펴볼까요?

( ① ) a year later, in October, London was startled by the unusually vicious murder of a respected, ( ② ) gentleman.

① **Nearly** [니얼리]가 아닌 [니어r을리]로 발음해 주세요.

② **elderly** [엘더r을리]로 발음해 주세요.

# 순간적으로 숨을 멈춰 보세요!

-ten, -ton, -tain으로 끝나는 단어는 t를 앞의 모음에 붙여서 발음하세요.

우리가 평소에 [버튼]으로 쉽게 발음하는 button, 하지만 원어민의 발음을 자세히 들어보면 [벝-은]으로 발음한다는 것을 알 수 있어요. 이처럼 -ten, -ton, -tain 등으로 끝나는 단어는 t를 앞의 모음에 붙인 다음 그 뒤는 순간적으로 숨을 멈추듯 [-은]으로 발음해 주어야 한답니다. 그럼 본문 49쪽과 54쪽에서 살펴볼까요?

It was (   ①   ) in an odd, upright style, and signed "Edward Hyde."

① **written** [리튼]이 아닌 [맅-은]이라고 발음하셨나요?

Mr. Guest's eyes (   ②   ), and he sat down at once and studied the letter with passion.

② **brightened** [브라잍-은ㄷ]라고 발음해 주세요.

# 지킬 박사와 하이드 씨

## 1장 | 문 이야기

**p.14~15** 변호사인 G. J. 어터슨 씨는 키가 크고 말랐다. 그는 자신에게 엄격했고 자신의 감정을 결코 드러내지 않았지만 조금은 사랑스러운 구석이 있었다. 그는 다른 사람들에게는 관대했고 곤란에 처한 사람들을 배척하기보다는 도우려는 사람이었다.

매주 일요일, 그는 가장 친한 친구인 리처드 엔필드와 오랜 산책을 했다. 엔필드는 어터슨 씨의 먼 사촌으로 유명한 풍류가였다. 두 사람의 성격은 너무 달랐기 때문에, 많은 사람들은 이 두 사람이 어떤 공통점을 가지고 있는지 궁금해했다. 사실 그들은 함께 있으면 편안함을 느꼈다.

어느 한 일요일 산책길에, 두 사람은 런던 번화가의 한 작은 거리를 지나게 되었다. 건물들은 깨끗하고 새로 페인트칠이 되어 있었다. 길 반대편 모퉁이에서 문 두 개를 지나면, 뜰로 들어가는 입구가 있었다.

**p.16~17** 그리고 그 바로 너머에는 2층 건물이 있었는데, 다른 모든 집들과는 달리 페인트칠이 필요했다. 아래층에 문이 하나 있었지만 길가 쪽으로 난 유리창은 없었다.

두 사람이 그 건물 가까이에 갔을 때, 엔필드가 지팡이를 들어 올리며 가리켰다.

"저 문을 보니 아주 이상한 이야기가 생각납니다." 그가 말했다.

"정말인가? 무슨 이야기인가?" 어터슨 씨가 말했다.

"새벽 세 시쯤 집으로 걸어오는 길이었는데 자그마한 남자가 길을 따라 서둘러 가고 있는 것을 보았습니다. 열 살쯤 되는 한 소녀가 최대한 가장 빠르게 골목길을 달려오고 있었어요. 모퉁이에서 두 사람은 부딪쳤고 소녀는 땅에 심하게 넘어져 비명을 지르기 시작했습니다. 그 다음에 일어난 일은 끔찍했어요. 그 남자는 소녀의 작은 몸을 조용히 짓밟고 갔어요. 저는 그의 뒤를 쫓아가서 붙잡았습니다. 남자는 무척 침착해 보였는데도, 추악하고 비열한 표정으로 저를 노려보았습니다.

p.18~19 저는 그의 목덜미를 잡아 비명을 지르는 소녀 옆에 가족이 모여 있는 곳으로 끌고 갔습니다. 잠시 후, 의사가 도착했고 소녀가 다치지는 않았다고 말하더군요. 소녀는 고통이 아닌 두려움으로 비명을 지른 것이었습니다. 저는 소녀가 두려워하는 이유를 전적으로 이해할 수 있었는데, 왜냐하면 제가 그 남자를 보자마자 그 사람이 싫어졌기 때문이었습니다. 그 아이의 가족도 모두 증오에 찬 표정으로 그를 노려보았지만, 가장 저의 흥미를 끈 것은 의사의 반응이었습니다. 그는 감정에 휩쓸리는 유형으로 보이지 않았지만, 나머지 우리들과 마찬가지로 제가 붙잡은 사람을 마치 죽이고 싶은 것처럼 바라보았습니다.

'그냥 빠져나갈 수는 없소. 만약 그렇게 한다면, 당신을 파멸시킬 추문을 만들 것이요.' 의사가 그에게 말했습니다.

'당연히 나는 추문을 피하고 싶소. 당신들이 이 일에 대해 잇어준다면, 아이에게 돈을 주겠소. 원하는 액수를 말해보시오.' 남자가 말했습니다.

p.20~21 우리는 100파운드를 요구했지만, 놀랍게도 그는 이의를 제기하지 않았습니다. 그는 저 문으로 걸어가서, 열쇠를 꺼내더니 안으로 사라졌습니다. 몇 분 후에 그는 금화 10파운드와 90파운드짜리 수표를 가지고 나왔습니다. 수표는 아주 유명한 사람의 이름으로 서명이 되어 있었습니다. 제가 수표의 서명이 그 유명한 사람의 것인지 믿지 못하겠다고 하자, 그는 아침까지 우리와 함께 있다가 직접 수표를 현금으로 바꿔 주겠다고 말했습니다. 그래서 의사와 소녀의 아버지, 저는 그 남자와 함께 저희 집에 가서 밤을 지새웠습니다. 다음 날 아침 일찍, 우리는 그 수표가 가짜일 것으로 내심 기대하며 그와 함께 은행으로 갔습니다. 놀랍게도, 그것은 진짜였습니다."

"이런. 그것 참 놀라운 이야기로군." 어터슨 씨가 말했다.

"네, 그렇습니다. 그리고 그는 끔찍하고 역겨운 사람입니다. 하지만 수표에 서명한 사람은 선한 사람이고 자선사업으로 잘 알려져 있습니다." 엔필드가 말했다.

"자네는 수표에 서명한 사람이 저기에 사는지 알고 있나?"

"아니요, 하지만 존경 받는 사람이 이런 낡은 곳에 살 가능성은 무척 낮을 것 같은데요, 그렇지 않습니까?" 엔필드가 말했다.

"그러면 자네는 저 문이 있는 집에 대해 그에게 물어보지는 않았나?" 어터슨 씨가 말했다.

"아니요, 그러지 않았습니다. 하지만 저곳을 살펴봤는데 저곳은 전혀 집 같지 않습니다. 다른 입구도 없고, 가끔 그 남자 말고는 저 문을 사용하는 사람도 없습니다. 2층에 뜰을 향해 난 창문이 세 개 있습니다. 아래층에는 창문이 하나도 없습니다. 2층의 창문들은 항상 닫혀 있습니다. 평상시에 굴뚝에서 연기가 나는 걸로 봐서 누군가가 저기에 사는 것 같습니다."

p.22~23  "훌륭한 관찰이네. 하지만 한 가지 물어 볼 게 있네. 그 소녀를 밟고 지나간 남자의 이름을 알고 있는가?" 어터슨 씨가 말했다.

"그의 이름은 하이드입니다." 엔필드가 말했다.

"음, 어떻게 생겼나?" 어터슨 씨가 말했다.

"그의 외모를 설명하기는 쉽지 않습니다. 이상해 보이는 남자입니다. 키는 작지만, 강하고 묵직한 몸을 가졌습니다. 그에게는 추하고 불쾌한 무언가가 있습니다. 저는 즉시 그가 싫어졌습니다."

"흥미롭군." 어터슨 씨가 말했다. "음, 리처드. 나는 수표에 서명한 사람을 알고 있네. 왜냐하면 전에 이 이야기를 좀 들었거든. 내게 말해준 것이 모두 확실한가?" 어터슨 씨가 말했다.

"그렇습니다." 엔필드가 말했다. "저는 모든 것을 일어난 그대로 설명했습니다. 하이드는 열쇠를 가지고 있었고, 아직도 가지고 있습니다. 왜냐하면 며칠 전에 그가 열쇠를 사용하는 것을 보았으니까요."

어터슨 씨는 한숨을 깊이 쉬며 아무 말도 하지 않았다.


### 2장 | 하이드 씨를 찾아서

p.26~27  어터슨 씨는 그날 저녁 식사를 하자마자, 사무실로 가서 금고를 연 다음 봉투 하나를 꺼냈다. 거기에는 헨리 지킬 박사의 유언장이 들어 있었다.

어터슨 씨는 책상에 앉아 서류를 읽었다. 거기에는 헨리 지킬이 사망하는 경우에, 지킬의 전 재산을 친애하는 친구인 에드워드 하이드에게 준다는 내용이 적혀 있었다. 그리고 지킬 박사가 3개월 이상 '실종 혹은 설명할 수 없는 부재'인 경우에도, 에드워드 하이드는 전 재산을 상속받게 되어 있었다. 어터슨 씨는 유산 상속의 조건이 적법하지 않은 건 아니지만 부자연스러우며 비도덕적이라고 생각했다. 그는 지킬이 이것을 쓰는 것에 도움을 주는 것을 거절했었다.

'나는 미친 짓이라고 생각했지. 하지만 지금 보니 이 유언장에 진정 흉악한 뭔가가 있는 게 틀림없어. 오늘 밤 친구 래니언 박사와 이 문제를 상의해 봐야겠어. 누군가 하이드에 대해 알고 있다면, 바로 그일 거야.' 어터슨 씨가 생각했다.

그는 두꺼운 외투를 걸치고 집을 나섰고 곧 캐번디시 광장에 있는 거대한 저택의 문을 두드리고 있었다. 집사가 문에서 어터슨 씨를 맞이하며 곧장 래니언 박사가 앉아 있는 식당으로 안내했다. 그는 굵은 백발의 건강하고 유쾌한 신사였다.

**p.28~29** 가벼운 대화 후에, 어터슨 씨는 마음에 담아둔 말을 하기 시작했다.

"자네와 헨리 지킬에 대해 이야기를 해야겠네. 우리 두 사람이 아마 그의 가장 오랜 친구들인 것으로 아는데, 그렇지 않은가?" 어터슨 씨가 말했다.

"그렇다고 생각하네." 래니언 박사가 말했다. "하지만 요즘에는 그를 자주 보지 못하네."

"그런가? 난 자네가 그와 공통의 관심사를 많이 가지고 있다고 생각했는데." 어터슨 씨가 말했다.

"한때는 공통점이 많았지. 하지만 헨리 지킬의 생각이 나에게 너무 공상적으로 보인 지도 10년이 넘었네. 그는 정신이 이상해지기 시작했고 말하는 것이 너무나 비과학적인 것들이어서 더 이상 그 친구 말을 참고 들어줄 수가 없었다네." 어터슨 씨가 말했다.

"하이드라고 불리는 지킬의 친구를 만나 본 적이 있는가?" 어터슨 씨가 물었다.

"하이드?" 래니언 박사가 반복했다. "아니. 그런 이름은 들어 본 적이 없네."

그날 밤 어터슨 씨는 마음이 복잡해서 잠을 이루지 못했다. 그는 엔필드의 충격적인 이야기와 지킬과 그의 피보호자인 하이드와의 관계에 얽힌 어지러운 꿈에 시달렸다. 이튿날 아침 교회 종이 6시를 칠 때에도, 여전히 그는 그 문제에 대해 생각하고 있었다. 그리고 그는 에드워드 하이드의 얼굴을 보고 싶은 호기심이 생겼다. 그를 한 번이라도 볼 수 있다면, 헨리 지킬의 유언장에 있는 이상한 조항의 이유를 이해할 수 있을 것 같았다. 그리고 친구인 엔필드가 왜 하이드를 보자마자 미워하게 됐는지도 알 수 있을 것 같았다.

p.30~31 그때부터 계속 어터슨 씨는 엔필드가 그에게 보여 주었던 문을 감시하기 시작했고, 마침내 맑고 서리가 내린 밤 10시에 그의 인내심이 보상을 받았다. 그가 몇 분 동안 문을 감시하고 있을 때 인도에서 가벼운 발자국 소리가 들렸다. 그는 뜰 입구의 어둠 속으로 한 걸음 물러섰다.

잠시 후에, 키가 작고 수수한 옷차림의 남자가 나타났고 어터슨 씨는 즉시 그에게 아주 강한 혐오감을 느꼈다. 그 남자는 문에 다가선 다음 주머니에서 열쇠를 꺼냈고, 그 순간 어터슨 씨가 어둠 속에서 나왔다.

"하이드 씨, 맞으시죠?" 어터슨은 그의 어깨를 툭 건드리며 말했다.

하이드 씨는 변호사 쪽으로 돌아보지 않고 조용히 대답했다.

"내 이름인데. 무엇 때문에 그러시오?"

"저는 지킬 박사의 오랜 친구로 제 이름을 들어 본 적이 있으실 겁니다." 변호사가 말했다. "제 이름은 어터슨입니다. 저를 안으로 초대해 줄 것이라 생각했는데요."

"여기서 지킬 박사를 만나지 못할 겁니다." 하이드 씨가 말했다.

"저도 압니다. 하지만 당신은 여기 산다고 들었습니다. 얼굴 좀 보여 주실 수 있습니까?" 어터슨 씨가 말했다.

p.32~33 하이드 씨는 잠시 망설이다가 몸을 돌려 변호사와 마주 보았다. 그들은 잠시 동안 서로를 뚫어져라 바라보았다.

"당신을 다시 만난다면 이제는 알아보겠소. 참고가 되겠군요." 변호사가 말했다.

"그렇군요. 이왕에 만났으니 내 집 주소도 알려 드리겠소."

그는 소호의 한 거리에 있는 집 주소를 변호사에게 알려주었다.

"나를 어떻게 알아본 거요?" 하이드 씨가 물었다.

"설명을 듣고 알았소. 우리는 이를테면 헨리 지킬과 같은 공통의 친구들이 있죠." 어터슨 씨가 말했다.

"거짓말하지 마시오!" 하이드가 화가 나서 소리쳤다. "우리는 공통의 친구가 없고 지킬이 당신에게 나에 대해 말했을 리가 없소!"

변호사가 대답을 하기도 전에, 하이드는 거칠고 비열한 웃음을 짓더니 집 안으로 사라졌다.

어터슨 씨는 하이드가 자리를 뜬 후에도 잠시 동안 서 있었다. 그는 초조했지만 그 이유는 알지 못했다. 그러고는 생각에 깊이 잠겨 천천히 길을 따라 걷기 시작했다. 그는 마침내 에드워드 하이드를 보았다. 남자는 창백하고 난쟁이처럼 작았다. 기형 같다는 인상을 풍겼지만, 어터슨 씨는 그 기형을 정확하게 본 것도 아니고 설명할 수도 없었다. 하이드 씨는 기분 나쁜 웃음을 짓고 목소리도 불쾌했지만, 이런 것들이 그에 대한 즉각적인 증오심을 설명해 주지는 않았다.

좁은 골목에서 모퉁이를 돌자 고풍스럽고 멋진 집들이 모여 있는 광장이 나왔다. 그 집들 중 많은 집들이 방치되어 있었지만, 한 집은 여전히 보존 상태가 좋았다. 어터슨 씨는 그 집 문 앞에서 걸음을 멈추고 문을 두드렸다. 나이가 지긋하고 옷을 잘 갖춰 입은 하인이 문을 열었다.

**p.34~35** "지킬 박사는 계신가, 풀?" 변호사가 물었다.

"안 계십니다, 변호사님. 박사님은 외출 중이십니다." 풀이 말했다.

"풀, 나는 하이드 씨가 낡은 실험동 문을 통해 안으로 들어가는 것을 보았네. 지킬 박사도 집에 없는데 그래도 괜찮은가?" 그가 말했다.

"네, 그렇습니다. 하이드 씨는 열쇠를 가지고 있고 그분의 명령을 따르라는 분부를 받았습니다." 집사가 대답했다.

"나는 하이드 씨를 한 번도 만난 적이 없는 것 같은데." 어터슨 씨가 말했다.

"맞습니다, 저희도 집 이쪽에서는 그를 거의 보지 못합니다. 그는 보통 실험동을 통해 출입합니다." 풀이 대답했다.

어터슨 씨는 그 어느 때보다 걱정을 많이 하며 집으로 걸어갔다.

2주일 후, 지킬 박사는 대여섯 명의 오랜 친구들을 유쾌한 저녁 식사에 초대했다. 어터슨 씨는 다른 사람들이 떠난 뒤에 혼자 남도록 조치를 취했다.

"자네 유언장에 대해 이야기를 하고 싶네, 지킬. 내가 그것에 대해 한 번도 찬성한 적이 없다는 것을 알 걸세." 변호사가 말했다.

"친구여. 자네는 불필요한 걱정을 하고 있어." 체격이 크고 건장한 50대의 지킬 박사가 말했다.

"그렇다면 다시 말하겠네. 나는 최근에 하이드에 대해서 안 좋은 이야기를 들었네." 변호사가 말했다.

p.36~37 지킬 박사의 잘생긴 얼굴이 창백해지고, 눈빛이 어두워졌다.

"자네가 무슨 이야기를 들었든지 상관 없네. 나는 말로는 바꿀 수 없는 이상하고 끔찍한 상황에 처해 있네." 그가 말했다.

"나를 믿게, 지킬. 자네의 상황에 대해서 이야기해 주게. 자네의 비밀이 무엇이든 지키겠네. 그리고 나는 분명히 자네를 그 상황에서 벗어나도록 할 수 있을 거야." 어터슨 씨가 말했다.

"친구여, 자네를 정말 믿고 이 세상 그 누구보다도 자네를 신뢰하네. 무엇이 잘못인지는 말할 수 없지만, 자네에게 한 가지는 약속하겠네. 나는 내가 원하면 언제든 하이드를 떨쳐낼 수 있네. 하지만 내가 하이드에게 매우 큰 관심을 가지고 있다는 것을 이해해 주길 바라네. 만약 나에게 무슨 일이 생기면, 내가 유언장에 남긴 것을 모두 그가 가질 수 있게 해 주게. 자네가 그를 도와주겠다고 약속해 준다면 내 마음이 편하겠네."

"그를 좋아하는 척은 할 수 없네." 변호사가 말했다.

"그걸 부탁하는 게 아니네." 지킬 박사가 말했다.

그는 일어서더니 어터슨 씨의 어깨에 손을 올렸다.

"내가 더 이상 여기에 없더라도, 나를 위해서 그를 도와주게." 지킬 박사가 말했다.

어터슨 씨는 한숨을 깊게 쉬었다.

"약속하겠네." 그가 말했다.

### 3장 | 커루 살인 사건

p.40~41 대략 일년이 지난 10월에, 존경 받는 노신사가 유례없이 잔인하게 살해된 사건으로 런던은 충격에 빠졌다. 강 가까이에 있는 집에서 혼자 사는 한 하녀가 범죄를 목격했다. 하녀는 11시쯤 창가에 앉아 있다가 백발의 노신사가 집 근처의 골목길을 따라 걸어오는 것을 보았다. 반대쪽에서 그를 향해 키가 아주 작은 한 신사가 걸어오고 있었는데, 하녀는 처음에는 그에게 관심을 두지 않았다. 두 사람이 마주쳤을 때, 노신사가 키가 작은 남자에게 정중하게 인사하며 길을 묻는 것처럼 보였다. 달빛이 노신사의 얼굴을 비추었고, 하녀는 노신사의 표정이 악의 없이 따뜻하다고 생각했다.

그러고 나서 그녀가 다른 신사를 보았을 때 그를 알아보고는 깜짝 놀랐다. 그는 하이드 씨로, 언젠가 자기 주인을 찾아온 적이 있었다. 그는 손에 무거운 지팡이를 들고 있었고 노신사의 말을 조바심을 내며 듣고 있는 것 같았다. 갑자기, 그는 불같이 화를 내며 발을 구르고 지팡이를 휘둘렀다.

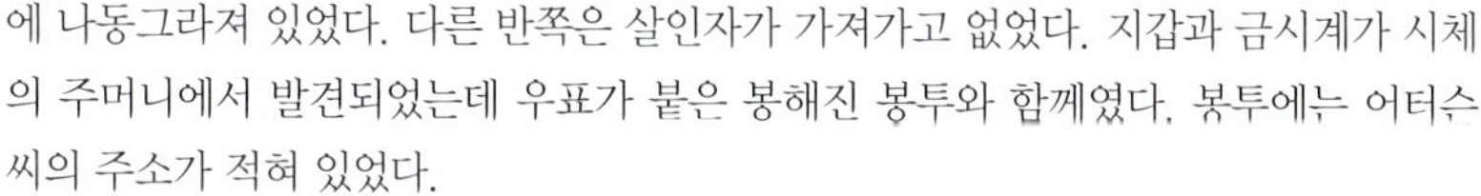

**p.42~43** 노신사가 한 걸음 뒤로 물러났다. 하이드 씨는 지팡이를 휘두르며 노신사의 몸을 후려치기 시작했고 하녀는 뼈가 으스러지는 소리를 들을 정도였다. 이 장면과 소리가 주는 공포에 못 이겨, 하녀는 기절을 하고 말았다.

하녀가 정신을 차리고 경찰을 부른 것은 2시가 되어서였다. 살인자는 오래 전에 사라지고 없었지만, 시체는 끔찍하게 뭉개져 길 한가운데에 놓여 있었다. 이 잔혹한 살인에 사용된 지팡이는 부러져 절반은 도랑에 나동그라져 있었다. 다른 반쪽은 살인자가 가져가고 없었다. 지갑과 금시계가 시체의 주머니에서 발견되었는데 우표가 붙은 봉해진 봉투와 함께였다. 봉투에는 어터슨 씨의 주소가 적혀 있었다.

편지는 그 다음 날 아침 일찍 변호사에게 전달되었다. 그는 살인 사건에 대해 듣자, 안색이 창백해졌다. 그는 시체가 옮겨져 있는 경찰서로 마차를 몰았고 시체를 보자마자 고개를 끄덕였다.

"누군지 알아보겠습니다. 유감스럽지만 이 분은 댄버스 커루 경입니다." 변호사가 말했다.

"이럴 수가!" 경찰관이 외쳤다. "아마 변호사님께서 커루 경을 이렇게 만든 자를 찾는 데 도움을 주실 수 있겠군요."

그리고 그는 하녀가 목격한 것을 간단하게 설명하고, 변호사에게 부러진 지팡이를 보여 주었다.

어터슨 씨는 하이드의 이름을 듣자 불안감이 엄습해 오는 것을 느꼈다. 하지만 그가 지팡이를 보았을 때, 하녀의 말이 맞다는 것을 깨달았다. 부러지긴 했지만, 그 지팡이는 몇 년 전에 자신이 헨리 지킬에게 준 것이라는 것을 알아보았기 때문이었다.

"저와 함께 가시죠. 하이드 씨가 사는 곳을 알고 있습니다." 어터슨 씨가 경찰관에게 말했다.

**p.44~45** 소호의 그 집 주소는 누더기를 걸친 아이들이 문 앞에 쭈그리고 앉아 있고, 초라한 옷차림의 여자들이 지저분한 가게 밖에서 가게 주인과 물건값을 흥정하느라

말싸움을 하고 있는 지저분한 거리에 있었다. 이곳이 바로 헨리 지킬의 젊은 친구가 사는 곳이었다. 어터슨 씨는 몸을 떨었다. 하이드 씨는 25만 파운드의 상속인이었다.

백발의 노파가 문을 열었다. 노파는 악한 얼굴을 하고 있었지만, 태도는 공손했다. 노파는 그들에게 하이드 씨가 이곳에 살고 있기는 하지만 집에 없다고 말했다. 그녀가 어제 그를 본 것도 거의 2개월 만의 일이었다.

"저와 같이 있는 이 신사분은 런던 경찰국의 뉴컴 경감입니다. 하이드 씨의 방을 보고 싶은데요." 어터슨 씨가 말했다.

하이드 씨는 집에서 방을 두 개만 사용하고 있었지만 방들은 고급스러운 취향의 가구들로 채워져 있었다. 찬장은 고급 와인으로 채워져 있었고, 벽에는 멋진 그림들이 걸려 있었다. 어터슨 씨는 이것이 미술 애호가인 헨리 지킬이 준 선물이라고 생각했다. 옷들은 바닥 여기저기에 널려 있었고 찬장 문들도 열려 있었다. 경감은 벽난로에서 타다 남은 잿더미에서 수표책을 찾았다. 문 뒤에는 부러진 지팡이의 나머지 절반이 있었다.

p.46~47 "잘 됐습니다! 이제 곧 그를 잡을 수 있겠어요. 자, 이제 은행에 가서 이 수표책의 주인에 대해 알아봅시다." 그가 어터슨 씨에게 말했다.

말할 것도 없이, 은행에는 에드워드 하이드의 이름으로 된 계좌에 수천 파운드가 있었다.

"이제 그를 잡았습니다!" 경감이 말했다. "우리는 살인 도구와 이 수표책을 확보했습니다. 사람은 돈 없이는 살 수 없습니다. 우리는 은행에서 그를 기다리기만 하면 됩니다. 이제 우리는 수배전단에 넣을 사진과 인물 설명만 있으면 됩니다."

하지만 수배전단에 넣을 하이드의 사진을 구할 수가 없었다. 그는 한 번도 사진이 찍힌 적이 없었다. 몇몇 사람들이 그의 생김새를 설명하려 했지만 그가 어쨌든 기형이라는 사실에 동의했을 뿐 의견이 일치되지 않았다. 하지만 하이드의 기형을 묘사해 달라고 하면, 아무도 설명하지 못했다.

그날 오후 늦게, 어터슨 씨는 지킬 박사의 집을 찾아갔다. 풀이 어터슨을 맞이해 지킬 박사의 사무실로 안내했다. 지킬 박사는 난롯가 옆에 앉아 있었고, 매우 아파 보였다. 그는 차가운 손을 친구를 향해 내밀고 기운 없는 목소리로 어터슨을 맞이했다.

p.48~49 "소식은 들었는가?" 둘만 남게 되자 어터슨 씨가 물었다.

"그렇다네, 신문팔이 소년들이 광장에서 외치고 있더군." 지킬 박사가 말했다.

"말해주게, 자네가 이자를 숨겨줄 만큼 정신이 나가진 않았겠지?" 어터슨 씨가 말했다.

"다시는 그를 만나지 않겠다고 하느님께 맹세하네. 내 명예를 걸고 그를 다시 만나지 않겠다고 약속하네. 그는 사라졌고 다시는 그로부터 소식을 들을 수 없을 것이네."

"자네는 그에 대해서 상당히 확신하는군. 자네 말이 옳기를 바라네. 만약 재판이 열린다면, 자네 이름이 언급될 수도 있어." 어터슨 씨가 말했다.

"나는 그에 대해 상당히 확신하네." 지킬 박사가 말했다. "다른 사람에게 말할 수는 없지만 확실한 근거가 있네. 하지만 자네가 조언을 해주었으면 하는 일이 하나 있네. 편지 한 통을 받았는데 이것을 경찰에게 보여주어야 하는지 모르겠네. 어터슨, 이것을 자네에게 맡기고 싶네. 자네가 현명하게 판단할 것이라 믿네. 그리고 나는 자네를 그만큼 많이 신뢰하고 있다네."

"그 편지를 보여 주게." 어터슨 씨가 말했다.

편지는 독특하고 똑바른 글씨체로 쓰여 있었고, '에드워드 하이드'라고 서명이 되어 있었다. 내용은 간단했고 친구이자 후원자인 지킬 박사에게 자신에 대해 걱정할 필요가 없다고 쓰여 있었다. 자기는 안전하며 절대 찾지 못할 것이고 지킬 박사의 관대함에 감사하며 이에 보답할 수 없을 것이라는 내용이었다.

p.50~51 "봉투는 가지고 있는가?" 어터슨 씨가 물었다.

"아무 생각 없이 태워 버렸네. 하지만 소인도 없었네. 편지는 인편으로 전달되었다네." 지킬 박사가 대답했다.

"내가 이것을 가져가서 밤새 생각해 보아도 되겠나?" 어터슨 씨가 물었다.

"그렇게 해주게. 전적으로 자네 판단에 맡기겠네. 나는 내 자신에 대한 믿음을 잃었다네." 지킬 박사가 말했다.

"생각해 보겠네." 변호사가 말했다. "그리고 하나만 더 물어보겠네. 자네 유언장에 자네의 행방불명에 대한 조항을 쓰도록 한 사람이 하이드가 맞나?"

지킬 박사는 입을 꽉 다물고 고개를 끄덕였다.

"그럴 줄 알았네. 그는 자네를 죽일 작정이었어. 자네는 겨우 목숨을 건진 거네." 어

터슨 씨가 말했다.

"나는 훨씬 중요한 것을 얻었네. 교훈을 얻었단 말이네. 오, 어터슨! 정말 중요한 교훈이지 뭔가!" 의사가 엄숙하게 말했다.

그리고 그는 잠시 동안 두 손으로 얼굴을 감쌌다.

나가는 길에, 변호사는 걸음을 멈추고 풀에게 말을 걸었다.

"오늘 지킬에게 인편으로 온 편지가 있다고 하던데. 편지를 전해 준 사람은 어떻게 생겼던가?"

"변호사님, 우체부 말고는 아무도 오지 않았는데요." 풀이 놀라서 말했다.

즉각 어터슨 씨의 공포가 다시 밀려왔다. 이 말은 편지가 실험동 문으로 전달되었거나 아니면 사무실에서 쓰여져서 지킬에게 남겨진 것이었다.

p.52~53  어터슨 씨가 지킬의 집을 나섰을 때, 신문팔이 소년들이 거리에서 머리기사를 외치고 있었다. "호외요! 댄버스 커루 경의 잔혹한 살인 사건에 대해서 읽어 보세요!"

'내 좋은 친구 댄버스 경의 슬프고도 충격적인 종말이 아닌가. 지킬 박사가 이 사건에 연루되지 않기만을 바라야겠군. 하지만 내가 이 편지를 어떻게 해야 할까?' 어터슨 씨가 생각했다.

그 생각이 스치자마자 그는 그 질문에 대답을 할 수 있는 사람이 누구인지 확실히 깨달았다.

그날 저녁 어터슨 씨는 사무장인 게스트와 난롯가에 앉았다. 어터슨 씨는 게스트를 전적으로 신뢰했고 그에게는 비밀이 거의 없었다. 게스트의 취미는 필체 연구였다.

p.54~55  "댄버스 경의 일은 정말 유감이네." 어터슨 씨가 말했다.

"정말 그렇습니다, 변호사님. 그 사건 때문에 여론이 들끓고 있습니다. 그런 짓을 한 사람은 물론 미친 거겠죠." 게스트가 말했다.

"그 문제에 대해 자네 의견을 듣고 싶네." 어터슨 씨가 말했다. "살인범의 필체로 쓴 문서가 여기 있네. 한번 읽어보게, 그리고 물론 이건 전적으로 자네와 나 둘만 아는 일이네."

게스트의 두 눈이 반짝이더니 즉시 열정적으로 편지를 살펴보았다.

"음, 변호사님, 이 편지를 쓴 사람은 미친 사람이 아니지만 무척 이상한 필체군요."
마침내 게스트가 말했다.

바로 그때, 하인이 메모를 들고 어터슨 씨에게 왔다.

"변호사님, 지킬 박사님에게 온 것입니까?" 게스트가 물었다. "그 필체를 알아보겠어요. 사적인 내용입니까?"

"아니, 저녁 식사 초대장일 뿐이네." 어터슨이 말했다. "이걸 보고 싶은가?"

"잠깐만 보겠습니다." 게스트가 말했다.

그는 두 장의 종이를 나란히 놓고 조심스럽게 두 종이의 필체를 비교했다.

"음, 변호사님." 마침내 게스트가 말했다. "두 종이에 쓰인 필체는 아주 유사합니다. 여러 면에서 동일한데, 하나는 오른쪽으로 기울었고 다른 하나는 똑바르다는 점만 빼고 말입니다."

"그것 참 이상하군. 게스트, 이 편지는 비밀이네."
어터슨 씨가 말했다.

"알겠습니다, 변호사님." 사무장이 말했다.

하지만 그날 밤 어터슨 씨는 혼자 있게 되자마자 금고 안에 편지를 집어 넣고 잠갔다.

'왜 헨리 지킬이 살인자를 위해서 편지를 위조해서 썼단 말인가?' 그는 의아했다.

그러자 두려움으로 온몸의 피가 얼어붙는 것 같았다.

## 4장 | 래니언 박사의 죽음

p.60~61 댄버스 경의 살인범을 잡기 위해 수천 파운드의 현상금이 내걸렸다. 하이드의 잔인함과 부도덕한 생활, 그리고 그의 괴이한 친구들에 대한 소문들이 전해졌지만, 그의 흔적을 찾을 수가 없었다. 그는 마치 존재한 적이 없었던 것처럼 사라졌다.

시간이 지나면서, 어터슨 씨는 자신이 발견한 놀랄만한 사건들이 가져다 준 열기에서 회복하기 시작했고 점차 마음의 평온을 되찾았다. 댄버스 경의 죽음은 비극이었지만 하이드의 실종으로 충분히 보상을 받았다고 그는 생각했다.

지킬 박사의 새로운 생활이 시작되었다. 그는 옛 친구들과의 우정도 되찾았고 다시 한 번 허물없고 환영 받는 손님이 되었다. 두 달이 넘게, 어터슨 씨는 거의 매일 지킬 박사를 만났고 그도 심적 조화를 이루고 있다고 느껴졌다.

1월 8일에, 어터슨 씨는 지킬 박사의 집에서 저녁 식사를 했다. 래니언 박사도 거기에 있었고 마치 세 사람이 떨어지고는 못 사는 친구들로 지냈던 그 옛날로 돌아간 것 같았다.

하지만 12일과 14일에, 지킬 박사는 어터슨을 만나기를 거절했다.

"박사님은 방 안에 틀어박혀 계십니다." 풀이 말했다.

그 다음 이틀 동안 이런 일이 계속되자 어터슨 씨는 점차 걱정이 되기 시작했다.

p.62~63 주말 저녁에, 어터슨 씨는 래니언 박사를 찾아갔고 항상 그랬던 것처럼 환영을 받았지만, 그의 갑자기 변해 버린 모습에 큰 충격을 받았다. 래니언 박사는 며칠 사이에 얼굴이 창백해지고, 체중도 줄고 눈에 띄게 늙고 머리숱도 줄어 있었다. 그는 마치 죽음을 눈앞에 둔 사람 같았다. 하지만 어터슨 씨가 래니언 박사에게 건강에 대해 묻자, 그는 두려움 없이 말했다.

"나는 충격을 받았다네." 래니언 박사가 솔직하게 말했다. "그리고 회복될 수 없을 거야. 내겐 몇 주 밖에 남지 않았네. 내 인생은 즐거웠고 나는 진정으로 그것을 즐겼네."

"지킬도 아프다네." 어터슨 씨가 말했다. "그를 만나 본 적이 있나?"

래니언 박사의 안색이 바뀌더니 떨리는 손을 들어 올렸다.

"다시는 지킬을 만나고 싶지도, 그에 대한 소식을 듣고 싶지도 않네." 래니언 박사는 떨리는 목소리로 말했다. "그와의 관계는 끝났고 나한테 그는 죽은 사람이나 다름없으니 내 앞에서 그 친구 이야기는 꺼내지 않도록 해주게나."

"세상에." 어터슨 씨가 말했다. "우리 셋은 아주 오랜 친구이지 않나, 래니언. 새로운 친구를 사귈 만큼 오래 살지도 못할 테고 말일세."

"자네가 할 수 있는 건 아무것도 없네." 래니언 박사가 말했다. "그에게 물어보게."

"지킬은 나를 집 안에 들이려 하지도 않네." 어터슨 씨가 말했다.

"놀라운 일도 아니군." 래니언 박사가 말했다. "언젠가 내가 죽고 나면, 자네도 이 일의 옳고 그름을 알게 될 걸세. 지킬에 대한 이야기는 하지 말아주게. 견딜 수가 없으니 말일세."

p.64~65 어터슨 씨는 집에 도착하자마자, 앉아서 지킬 박사에게 편지를 썼다. 편지에서 그는 왜 자신을 집에 들이지 않는지 그리고 래니언 박사와 왜 사이가 틀어졌는지를 물었다.

다음 날, 어터슨 씨는 지킬 박사의 답장을 받았다.

'래니언과의 다툼은 돌이킬 수 없네. 그를 탓하는 것은 아니지만, 래니언과 나는 다시는 만나서는 안 된다는 점에 동의하네. 나는 이제부터 고독한 삶을 살려고 하네. 우리 집 문이 자네한테조차 굳게 닫힌다 하더라도, 놀라거나 나의 우정을 의심해서는 안 되네. 나는 나 스스로를 끔찍한 위험에 빠뜨렸고 지금 그에 대한 벌을 받고 있다네. 내가 내 죄로 인해 고통을 받고 있다는 사실 외에는 자네에게 더 이상 아무 것도 말해 줄 수가 없네. 나의 침묵을 존중해 주게. 자네가 나를 위해서 해줄 수 있는 것은 아무것도 없네.' 지킬은 이렇게 썼다.

몇 주 후, 래니언 박사는 병석에 누웠고 2주일도 안 돼 세상을 떠났다. 장례식을 치른 날 밤, 어터슨 씨는 개인 금고에서 봉인된 봉투를 꺼냈다. 봉투에는 래니언의 필체로 이렇게 쓰여 있었다. '*비밀 문서. G. J. 어터슨만이 열어 볼 것.*'

변호사는 봉인을 뜯었다. 안에는 봉인된 또 다른 봉투가 들어 있었다. 그 위에는 이렇게 쓰여 있었다. '*헨리 지킬 박사가 죽거나 행방불명이 되기 전에 열어 보아서는 안 됨.*'

p.66~67 어터슨 씨는 깜짝 놀랐다. 이것은 오래 전에 지킬에게 돌려 주었던 그 정신 나간 유언장에 있던 것과 같은 말이다. 하지만 래니언이 쓴 저 말들은 무슨 의미였을까? 그는 무엇을 알고 있었을까? 변호사는 궁금한 나머지 봉투를 열어 이 수수께끼들을 풀고만 싶었다. 하지만 직업상의 명예와 죽은 친구와의 약속이 너무 강했다. 이 봉투는 그 조건들이 충족될 때까지 개인 금고에 있을 것이었다.

몇 주 뒤 일요일의 산책에서, 어터슨 씨와 엔필드는 어느덧 둘 다 하이드를 만난 적이 있는 작은 골목길에 이르게 되었다.

"어쨌든 적어도 그 이야기는 끝이 났군요. 하이드를 다시는 보지 못하겠군요." 엔필드가 말했다.

"그러지 않기를 바라네." 어터슨 씨가 말했다. "여기서 하이드를 한 번 만난 적이 있고 자네가 느꼈던 그 혐오감을 나도 느꼈다고 이야기했던가?"

"그에게 혐오감을 느끼지 않을 수는 없을 겁니다. 그런데 이 문이 지킬 박사님의 집으로 통하는 길이라는 것도 모르고 있었으니 저를 멍청하다고 생각하지 않으셨나요?" 엔필드가 말했다.

p.68~69 "그럼 자네도 알아냈단 말인가? 그렇다면 뜰로 들어가서 창문들을 살펴보세. 나는 불쌍한 지킬이 걱정되어 바깥이긴 하지만 친구가 있으면 그에게 위로가 될지도 모른다는 생각이 든다네." 어터슨 씨가 말했다.

거리는 밝고 햇살이 있었지만, 뜰은 축축하고 그늘이 져 있었다. 지킬 박사 사무실의 가운데 창문이 반쯤 열려 있었고 지킬 박사가 그 옆에 앉아 있었다. 그의 얼굴은 석방을 간절히 바라는 죄수와 같은 슬픈 표정을 짓고 있었다.

"지킬! 놀라운 일이군! 몸이 나아지고 있기를 바라네." 어터슨 씨가 외쳤다.

"나는 몸이 무척 좋지 않네." 지킬 박사가 대답했다. "이게 오래 지속되지는 않을 걸세. 다행이지."

"자네는 집 안에 너무 오랫동안 있었네. 밖으로 나와서 운동이라도 좀 하게. 어서, 모자를 가지고 우리와 잠시 산책을 하세." 변호사가 말했다.

"나도 그러고 싶지만 불가능하네. 하지만 자네를 보니 정말 반갑네, 어터슨. 자네와 엔필드를 안으로 초대하고 싶지만 손님이 들어오기에는 이곳이 너무 누추하네."

p.70~71 "음, 그렇다면 우리가 여기 아래에서 잠시 자네와 얘기를 하는 것이 어떻겠나?" 어터슨 씨가 말했다.

"안 그래도 나도 막 똑같은 것을 제안하려던 참이었네." 지킬이 희미한 미소를 지으며 말했다.

하지만 그가 말을 채 마치자마자 그의 미소가 공포와 절망의 표정으로 바뀌었다. 어터슨 씨와 엔필드는 창문이 닫히기 전에 아주 잠깐 동안 그의 얼굴을 보았지만, 그 짧은 순간만으로도 그들의 등골을 오싹하게 하기에 충분했다. 그들은 뒤돌아서 빠르게 걸었고, 골목길에서 한참 멀어지고 나서야 어터슨 씨는 입을 열었다.

"하느님, 저희를 도와주소서!" 그는 공포에 질려 말했다.

하지만 엔필드는 너무 겁에 질려 고개만 끄덕였을 뿐 아무 말없이 걸었다.

`p.74~75`  어느 날 저녁, 풀이 어터슨 씨를 찾아왔다.

"이런! 풀, 여기까지 웬일인가? 지킬이 아픈가?" 그가 말했다.

"변호사님, 뭔가 잘못되었습니다." 풀이 말했다.

"여기 앉게. 와인을 한 잔 따라 주겠네." 변호사가 말했다. "서두를 것 없네. 무슨 일이 일어났는지 말해보게."

"변호사님도 박사님의 습관을 잘 아시죠. 스스로를 가두고 계신 것도요. 지금 박사님은 서재에 틀어박혀 계십니다. 변호사님, 저는 그게 너무 두렵고 더 이상 견딜 수가 없습니다." 풀이 말했다.

"자네가 두려워하는 것이 정확하게 무엇인지 말해보게." 어터슨 씨가 말했다.

풀은 한 번도 어터슨의 얼굴을 바라보지 않았다. 그의 눈은 바닥을 보고 있었다.

"말해보게. 뭔가 아주 잘못되었다는 것은 나도 알고 있네. 그게 무엇인지 말 좀 해보게." 어터슨 씨가 말했다.

"범죄가 일어난 것 같습니다." 풀이 쉰 목소리로 말했다.

"범죄라고!" 변호사가 외쳤다. "그게 무슨 말인가?"

"말씀드릴 수 없습니다, 변호사님. 저와 함께 가서 직접 보시겠습니까?" 풀이 말했다.

`p.76~77`  어터슨 씨가 모자와 외투를 가지러 가자 집사의 얼굴에 안도의 표정이 나타났다. 바람이 거세게 불고 달빛이 어슴푸레하게 비치는 밤이었고, 바람이 휩쓸고 지나간 것처럼 평소와는 달리 거리에는 사람들이 거의 없었다.

그들이 지킬 박사의 집에 도착하자, 풀이 가볍게 문을 두드렸다. 안전 사슬이 걸린 채 문이 약간 열렸다.

"풀, 집사님이세요?" 목소리가 들렸다.

"맞네. 문을 열게." 풀이 말했다.

그들은 벽난로에 불이 타고 있어 환하게 밝혀진 응접실로 들어갔다. 하인들이 모두 모여 있었다.

어터슨을 보자 요리사가 외쳤다. "다행이다! 변호사님이 오셨어."

“왜 모두들 여기 있는 건가?” 변호사가 말했다.

“저들은 모두 두려워하고 있습니다.” 풀이 말했다.

침묵이 흘렀고 하녀가 큰 소리로 울기 시작했다.

“조용히 하게!” 풀이 하녀에게 화를 내며 말했다.

그러고 나서 그는 어터슨 씨를 뒷마당으로 안내했다.

“변호사님, 이제부터 최대한 조용히 하셔야 합니다. 소리를 들으시는 건 되지만 소리를 내서서는 안 됩니다. 그리고 그가 변호사님에게 들어오라고 해도, 들어가시면 안 됩니다.” 풀이 말했다.

p.78~79 어터슨 씨는 집사를 따라 실험동 건물로 들어갔다. 사무실로 통하는 계단 아래에서, 그들은 멈췄다. 그리고 풀은 계단을 올라가 문을 두드렸다.

“박사님, 어터슨 씨가 뵙기를 원하십니다.” 풀이 말했다.

“그에게 아무도 만날 수 없다고 전해 주게.” 애처로운 목소리가 들렸다.

“고맙습니다, 박사님.” 풀은 이렇게 말하고는 어터슨 씨를 인도해 마당을 다시 지나 부엌으로 갔다.

“선생님, 저게 우리 주인님의 목소리였습니까?” 풀이 어터슨 씨의 눈을 보며 말했다.

“많이 변한 것 같은데.” 변호사가 대답했다.

“변한 것 같다고요? 저는 이 집에서 20년 동안 일해 왔습니다. 저는 제 주인님의 목소리를 알고 있고 사무실에서 나는 목소리는 주인님의 것이 아닙니다. 주인님은 8일 전에 사라지셨어요. 우리는 주인님이 하느님의 이름을 부르며 울부짖는 소리를 들었고 그 이후로는 목소리를 듣지 못했습니다. 사무실에 있는 자도 하느님의 자비를 구하더군요.”

“참 이상하군.” 어터슨 씨가 말했다. “만약 지킬이 살해되었다면, 왜 살인범이 그곳에 있겠는가? 그건 말이 안 되네.”

“음, 어터슨 씨.” 풀이 말했다. “일주일 동안, 방에 있는 저자가 약을 구하려고 밤낮으로 울부짖었습니다. 주인님은 가끔씩 종이에 지시 사항을 써서 제가 가져가도록 계단에 두셨습니다. 하지만 이번 주에는 쪽지가 매일 있고 문은 계속 닫혀 있습니다. 저는 시내에 있는 모든 도매 약제상을 찾아 다니며 주문한 약을 가져왔습니다. 매번 불순물이 섞여 있으니 되돌려 주고 다른 회사에 주문을 하라고 적혀 있는 쪽지를 받았습니다. 변호사님, 저자는 그 약을 간절히 원하고 있습니다.”

p.80~81 “그 쪽지들 중 가지고 있는 게 있나?” 어터슨 씨가 물었다.

풀은 주머니에서 구겨진 쪽지를 하나 꺼내 변호사에게 주었다.

어터슨 씨가 읽었다.

> 모우 상회 귀하. 지킬 박사로부터.
> 마지막 견본은 불순물이 섞여 있습니다. 몇 년 전에, 지킬 박사가 귀사에서 대량으로 구입한 적이 있습니다. 좀더 주의 깊게 다시 찾아봐 주시고 똑같은 품질의 약이 발견되면, 즉시 박사에게 보내 주십시오. 가격은 중요하지 않습니다. 지킬 박사가 이 약이 급하게 필요합니다. 부디 이전의 약을 조금이라도 구해 주십시오.

“이상한 쪽지군.” 어터슨 씨가 말했다. “자네가 어떻게 열어 본 건가?”

“모우 상회의 직원이 화가 나서 저에게 던져 버렸습니다.” 풀이 말했다.

“이건 틀림없이 지킬의 필체로군, 그렇지 않나?” 변호사가 말했다.

“그렇다고 생각했습니다. 그런데 왜 필체에 신경을 쓰십니까? 저는 그자를 봤다고요!” 풀이 말했다.

“그자를 봤다고? 무엇을 봤다는 말인가?” 어터슨 씨가 말했다.

“저는 그자를 봤습니다.” 풀이 말했다. “제가 정원에서 실험동으로 들어가는데 그자가 안에서 상자들을 뒤지고 있었습니다. 제가 들어가자 고개를 들더니 소리를 지르면서 계단을 뛰어올라가 사무실로 들어가는 것이었습니다. 제가 그자를 본 것은 아주 잠깐이었지만, 두려움으로 머리카락이 곤두섰습니다. 변호사님, 그자가 제 주인님이었다면, 왜 가면을 쓰고 있었겠습니까? 그자가 제 주인님이라면, 왜 쥐처럼 소리를 지르며 저에게서 달아났을까요?”

“이 모든 것이 정말 이상하군.” 어터슨 씨가 말했다. “내 생각에 자네 주인은 고통과 기형을 동반하는 병에 걸린 것이네. 목소리가 변한 것과 가면을 쓴 것, 그리고 친구들을 피하는 이유도 설명이 되네. 그리고 그것이 지킬이 이 약을 찾는데 그렇게 혈안이 되어 있는 이유지.”

p.82~83 “변호사님.” 풀이 말했다. “그자는 우리 주인님이 아니었습니다. 주인님은 키가 크고 체격이 좋은데, 그자는 오히려 난쟁이에 가까웠습니다. 가면을 쓴 자는 지킬 박사님이 아니었습니다. 저는 살인이 일어났다고 생각합니다.”

"그것이 사실이라면, 이 일을 분명하게 짚고 넘어가는 것이 내 의무네. 자네가 지킬이 무슨 해를 당했다고 생각한다면, 나는 저 문을 부수고 들어가겠네. 누가 나를 돕겠나?"

"변호사님, 제가 하겠습니다." 풀이 용감하게 말했다. "저는 실험실에서 도끼를 가져 갈 테니 변호사님은 부지깽이를 가져 가십시오."

변호사는 투박하고 묵직한 부지깽이를 손에 쥐었다.

"이 일로 자네와 내가 아주 위험한 상황에 처할 수도 있다는 것을 아는가?" 변호사가 물었다.

"네, 압니다. 변호사님." 집사가 대답했다.

"그렇다면 우리 솔직해지세. 자네가 봤다는 가면을 쓴 자를 알아보았는가?" 어터슨 씨가 말했다.

"그자는 아주 빨리 움직였습니다." 풀이 말했다. "하지만 그자가 하이드 씨였는지를 묻고 계시는 거죠? 네, 그자는 체격도 비슷하고 움직이는 모습도 같았습니다. 그리고 그자가 사라졌을 때 열쇠를 가지고 있었기 때문에 실험동 문으로 들어올 수도 있었을 겁니다. 하지만 그것이 다는 아닙니다. 변호사님은 하이드 씨를 만나 본 적이 있으십니까?"

"그렇다네. 한 번 이야기를 해 본 적이 있네." 어터슨 씨가 말했다.

p.84~85 "그러시다면 선생님께서도 그 사람에게 뭔가 기괴한 점이 있다는 것을 아시겠군요." 풀이 말했다. "사람을 오싹하게 만드는 구석이 있다는 것을 말입니다."

"맞아. 나도 자네가 말하는 그런 느낌을 받았네." 어터슨 씨가 말했다.

"가면을 쓴 그자가 사무실로 뛰어 들어갔을 때 저도 같은 것을 느꼈습니다." 풀이 말했다. "어터슨 씨, 그것이 증거가 될 수 없다는 것을 압니다. 하지만 그자가 하이드였다는 것을 맹세하겠습니다."

"맞네. 유감스럽지만 자네 말이 맞는 것 같네." 변호사가 말했다.

어터슨 씨는 다른 두 하인에게 몽둥이를 들고 실험실 문 가까이에 서 있으라고 말했다.

"누군가 나오려고 하면, 그들을 막게." 그가 말했다.

겨드랑이에 부지깽이를 끼고, 변호사는 그들이 앉아서 기다릴 실험실로 갔다. 사무실에서 서성대는 발걸음 소리를 들을 수 있었다.

"하루 종일 서성거립니다." 풀이 속삭였다. "약제상에서 새로운 견본이 올 때만 걸음을 멈춥니다. 하지만 말씀해 주십시오. 저것이 박사님의 발걸음 소리입니까?"

발걸음 소리는 가볍고 느렸다. 헨리 지킬의 무거운 발걸음 소리와는 무척이나 달랐다.

어터슨 씨는 한숨을 쉬며 말했다. "아니네. 뭔가 또 다른 것은 없나?"

풀은 고개를 끄덕였다. "우는 소리를 들은 적이 있습니다!"

"울었다고?" 변호사는 공포감을 느끼면서 말했다.

"마치 지옥에 떨어진 영혼처럼 울더군요." 집사가 말했다. "그 소리에 마음이 무거워져서 저까지 울고 싶어졌습니다."

풀은 도끼를 집어 들고 탁자 위에 촛불을 내려 놓았다. 그들은 계단을 올라가서 사무실 문 밖에 멈춰 섰다.

"지킬." 어터슨 씨가 소리쳤다. "자네를 만나야겠네!"

잠시 기다렸지만, 아무런 대답이 없었다.

"만약 자네가 문을 열지 않으면, 이 문을 부수겠네." 그가 말했다.

"어터슨, 제발, 자비를 베풀어 주게!" 목소리가 들려왔다.

"저건 지킬의 목소리가 아니야! 하이드의 목소리야! 풀, 문을 부수게!" 어터슨 씨가 외쳤다.

p.86~87 풀이 도끼로 문을 내리치자, 사무실 안에서 비명 소리가 들렸다. 도끼로 문을 반복해서 내리쳤고 다섯 번을 내리치고서야, 자물쇠가 산산이 부서지고 문의 잔해가 방 안 양탄자 위로 떨어졌다.

어터슨 씨와 풀은 사무실 안을 살펴보았다. 불이 환하게 켜져 있고 벽난로에는 불이 타고 있어 따뜻했다. 책상 위에 서류들이 가지런히 쌓여 있었고 벽난로 가까이에 쟁반이 놓여 있었다. 방 한가운데에 꿈틀거리는 한 남자의 몸이 바닥에 엎드려 있었다. 어터슨 씨는 조심스럽게 방으로 걸어가서, 몸을 굽혀 남자의 몸을 뒤집었다. 그는 에드워드 하이드였다. 그는 체구에 비해 너무 큰 옷을 입고 있었고 손에는 작은 약병을 쥐고 있었다.

어터슨 씨는 자신이 자살한 사람의 시체를 보고 있다는 것을 깨달았다.

"우리는 그를 구하기에도 벌주기에도 너무 늦었네. 그는 죽었네. 이제 자네 주인의 시체를 찾아보세." 어터슨 씨가 말했다.

그들은 사무실과 실험실을 주의 깊게 살펴보았지만 살았든 죽었든 헨리 지킬의 흔적은 없었다. 풀은 실험실 바닥의 넓은 돌을 쿵쿵 밟아 보았다.

p.88~89  "아마 여기에 묻혀 있겠죠." 풀이 말했다.

"아니면 도망쳤을지도 모르지." 어터슨 씨가 말했다.

그들은 계단을 다시 올라가 사무실의 물건들을 주의 깊게 살펴보기 시작했다. 탁자에는 계량된 여러 뭉치의 하얀 가루가 유리 접시 위에 놓여 있었다. 하이드는 무슨 실험을 준비하고 있었던 것처럼 보였다.

"저것이 제가 항상 그자에게 가져다 준 것과 같은 약입니다." 풀이 말했다.

다음으로 그들은 책상을 살펴보았다. 깔끔하게 정돈되어 있는 서류들 위에 커다란 봉투가 있었다. 봉투에는 지킬 박사의 필체로 어터슨의 이름이 쓰여 있었다. 변호사가 봉투를 열자 동봉된 것들이 바닥에 떨어졌다. 첫 번째 서류는 유언장이었다. 거기에는 6개월 전에 어터슨 씨가 지킬 박사에게 돌려주었던 것과 같은 이상한 조항과 조건들이 들어 있었다.

하지만 그는 에드워드 하이드의 이름 대신 가브리엘 존 어터슨의 이름이 있는 것을 보고 무척 놀랐다.

그는 서류들을 본 다음, 바닥에 있는 시체를 바라보았다.

"머리가 어지럽군." 어터슨 씨가 말했다. "하이드는 지킬의 유언장에서 자신의 이름이 빠진 것을 보고 격분했을 텐데. 그래도 이것을 며칠이나 그대로 가지고 있으면서 없애지 않았다니."

p.90~91  그는 다음 서류를 집어 들었다. 그것은 지킬 박사의 필체로 쓰인 짧은 쪽지였고 윗부분에 날짜가 쓰여 있었다.

"풀!" 어터슨 씨가 말했다. "그는 살아 있었고 오늘 이 쪽지를 썼네. 이렇게 짧은 시간에 사람을 죽이고 시체까지 처리한다는 것은 불가능하네. 그는 아직 살아 있고 도망간 것이 분명하네. 우리 둘 다 신중해야 하네. 자네 주인을 이런 비극에 개입시키는 것을 원하지 않으니 말이네."

"변호사님, 그 쪽지를 읽어 보지 그러십니까?" 풀이 물었다.

"지킬이 쓴 것일지도 몰라서 두렵네." 어터슨이 엄숙하게 대답했다. 그러고 나서 그는 쪽지를 읽었다.

친애하는 어터슨에게

이 편지가 자네 수중에 들어갔을 때면, 나는 사라지고 없을 걸세. 그 일이 어떤 식으로 일어날지 모르지만, 내 직감으로 파국은 확실히 그리고 곧 닥칠 것이 분명하네. 먼저, 래니언이 자네에게 준 편지를 읽어 보게. 그러고 나서 하찮고 불행한 자네 친구의 고백을 읽게나.

헨리 지킬

"또 다른 서류가 있을 서야." 어터슨 씨가 말했다.

"여기 있습니다, 변호사님." 풀이 말하며 그에게 크고 묵직한 봉투를 건넸다. 변호사는 그것을 주머니에 넣었다.

"풀, 이것에 대해서 아무 말도 하지 말게." 그가 말했다. "지금은 10시고 나는 집에 가서 이 서류들을 읽어 보아야겠네. 자정 전에 돌아올 테니 그때 경찰을 부르러 사람을 보내세."

그들은 실험실 문을 잠그고 밖으로 나왔다. 어터슨 씨는 무거운 마음으로 두 통의 편지가 이 수수께끼를 설명할 수 있기를 바라며 집으로 걸어갔다.

## 6장 | 래니언 박사의 편지

p.94~95  어터슨 씨는 사무실로 들어가 문을 잠갔다. 그러고 나서 책상에 앉아 래니언 박사의 장례식 날에 받은 봉투를 뜯었다. 그는 읽기 시작했다.

나흘 전, 1월 9일 저녁에 헨리 지킬 박사의 필체로 주소가 쓰여진 봉투가 나에게 배달되었네. 우리는 서로 편지를 쓰는 사이도 아니었고 그 전날 함께 저녁을 먹은 터라 편지를 받고 무척 놀랐네. 나는 편지의 내용을 읽고 더욱 놀랐네. 지킬이 쓴 내용은 다음과 같네.

친애하는 래니언에게

자네는 나의 가장 오랜 벗 중 한 명이고 과학과 관련된 문제로 의견을 달리한 적이 있었을지는 몰라도, 우리의 우정에 금이 간 적은 없었다고 생각되네. 오늘 밤, 내 목숨, 내 명예와 온전한 정신이 모두 자네 손에 달려 있네. 자네가 나를 저버린다면, 나는 끝장이네.

제발 오늘 밤 다른 모든 약속을 미뤄주게. 마차를 타고 이 편지를 가지고 우리 집으로 가게.

집사인 풀이 열쇠공과 함께 자네를 기다리고 있을 걸세. 열쇠공에게 내 사무실 문을 열도록 하게. 안으로 혼자 들어가서 왼편에 E라고 표시가 된 찬장을 열게. 위에서 네 번째 서랍을 열면 종이에 싸인 가루와 조그만 유리병, 공책 한 권이 들어 있을 것이네. 이 서랍과 그 안에 들어 있는 것들을 가지고 자네 집으로 돌아가 주게.

**p.96~97** 부탁이니 자정에 자네 진료실에 혼자 있게. 한 남자가 자네를 만나러 갈 것이네. 그에게 그 서랍을 주게. 자네가 굳이 설명을 필요로 한다면, 5분 후에 설명을 들을 수 있을 것이네.

자네가 나를 실망시키지 않을 것이라는 것을 알고 있네. 지금 이 순간에 낯선 곳에서 엄청난 고통을 받고 있는 나를 생각해 주게. 내가 부탁한 대로 해 준다면, 내 문제들은 금새 해결될 것이네. 친애하는 래니언, 나를 도와 주게.

자네의 친구,<br>
H. 지킬

P.S. 이 편지가 내일 아침까지 도착하지 않는다 해도 가능한 한 빨리 내가 부탁한 일을 해 주게. 그리고 나서 내일 자정에 내가 보낸 사람을 기다려 주게. 내일 자정에도 내가 보낸 사람이 가지 않고 그냥 지나간다면, 자네는 헨리 지킬의 최후를 보게 될 것이네.

나는 이 편지를 읽고 나서, 지킬이 미쳤다고 확신했지만 의심의 여지 없이 그것이 증명될 때까지는, 지킬이 부탁한 대로 하는 것이 내 의무라고 생각했네. 나는 마차를 잡아 타고 곧바로 그의 집으로 갔네. 집사가 열쇠공과 함께 나를 기다리고 있었네. 나는 그가 지시한 대로, 찬장에서 서랍을 빼내 종이에 싸서 집으로 돌아왔네.

p.98~99 나는 진료실에서 내용물들을 살펴보았네. 포장지에는 보통의 하얀 소금 같은 것이 있었네. 병에는 피처럼 붉은 액체가 반쯤 차 있었는데 인과 에테르의 강한 냄새가 났네. 공책은 몇 년에 걸쳐 일련의 날짜들이 기록되어 있었는데, 1년 전쯤부터 갑자기 기록이 중단되었더

군. 나는 그 공책이 성공하지 못한 실험의 기록들이라고 생각했네.

지킬이 왜 나를 이 일에 끌어들였는지에 단서가 될 만한 것은 없었다네. 그가 보낸 사람도 그의 지시를 따를 수 있었을 텐데 말이네. 그리고 나는 왜 그가 보낸 사람을 몰래 만나야 하는지? 생각하면 할수록, 나는 정신병자의 사건을 다루고 있다는 확신이 더 들었네.

p.100~101 12시에, 문을 두드리는 소리가 났네. 문을 열자 작은 남자가 현관 기둥에 기대어 웅크리고 있는 것을 발견했네. 나는 그를 안으로 들어오도록 했네. 진료실은 불이 환하게 켜져 있어서 나는 남자를 똑똑히 볼 수 있었다네. 그는 키가 작고 근육질에 얼굴에는 매우 불쾌한 표정을 짓고 있었네. 그는 쇠약하고 아파 보였지만 보자마자 아주 강한 혐오감이 들었네.

그의 옷은 질 좋고 비싼 천으로 만든 것이었지만 그에게 너무 컸네. 바지는 땅에 끌리지 않도록 말아 올려졌고, 외투의 허리는 엉덩이에 걸려 있었네. 외투의 깃은 거의 어깨만큼 넓었다네. 하지만 나는 그를 보고 웃음이 나오지 않았네. 그에게는 뭔가 괴상하고 불쾌한 것이 있었네.

"가져왔소?" 그자가 외쳤네.

그는 조바심을 내며 내 팔에 손을 얹기까지 했네. 그가 손을 대자 한기가 느껴져 나는 그를 뿌리쳤네.

"잘 오셨습니다. 괜찮으시다면 앉으세요." 나는 말했다네.

"죄송합니다, 래니언 박사님." 그가 대답했네. "제가 참을성이 없어 무례를 범했습니다. 저는 헨리 지킬 박사의 부탁을 받고 중요한 일로 여기에 왔습니다. 저에게 주실 것을 가지고 계신 것으로 알고 있는데요."

p.102~103 "저기 있습니다, 선생님." 나는 말하면서 바닥에 있는 종이로 싸여진 서랍을 가리켰네.

그는 마치 고통스러운 것처럼 심장에 손을 갖다 대었네. 그러더니 서랍으로 가서 종이를 잡아 당겼네. 그 안에 든 것을 보더니, 그는 엄청난 안도감에 큰 소리로 흐느껴서 나는 충격을 받았네.

"계량컵이 있습니까?" 그가 물었네.

내가 계량컵을 갖다 주자 그는 붉은색 혼합물 소량을 재어서 덜어내더니 거기에 가루를 넣었네.

가루가 용해되면서 혼합물의 색깔이 선명해지기 시작했네. 그러자 거품이 나기 시작하더니 증기가 생겼네. 갑자기 거품이 생기는 것이 멈추더니 짙은 자주빛으로 변했네. 그러더니 천천히 연녹색으로 옅어졌네. 방문객은 미소를 띠며 책상 위에 계량컵을 올려 놓았네.

"그러면 이제 남은 일을 처리해야겠군. 당신이 내게 이 계량컵을 들고 당신 집을 떠나라고 한다면, 당신의 삶은 변하지 않을 것이오. 하지만 나를 여기 있게 한다면, 당신은 새로운 지식과 명성을 얻게 될 것이오. 당신은 사탄이나 신의 힘에 대적하는 기적을 보게 될 테니까 말이오." 그가 말했다.

p.104~105 "선생님. 수수께끼 같은 말을 하시는군요. 그리고 나는 결코 기적을 믿지 않습니다. 하지만 나는 친구를 위해서 알 수 없는 부탁을 들어주었고 이제 결말을 보기 전에는 멈출 수 없소." 내가 차분하게 말했네.

"그렇다면 지금부터 일어나는 일은 우리의 직업을 걸고 비밀에 부치겠다고 약속하시오. 당신은 항상 편협한 관점을 가지고 있었지만, 이 기적을 잘 보시오!"

그는 계량컵을 입술로 가져가더니 내용물을 단숨에 마셔 버렸네. 그는 비명을 지르더니 비틀거리면서 탁자를 꽉 붙잡더군. 그는 탁자에 계속 매달린 채 입을 벌리고 숨을 헐떡거리며 노려보았다네. 그리고 내가 보는 동안, 그는 몸이 부풀어 오르는 것 같았네. 그의 얼굴은 검어지고, 이목구비가 녹고 바뀌는 것 같았네. 나는 벽에 몸을 기대고 그자로부터 나를 보호하려고 팔을 들어 올렸네.

p.106~107 "오, 하느님! 오, 하느님!" 나는 계속해서 비명을 질렀네.

헨리 지킬이 내 앞에 서 있었네. 그는 창백한 얼굴로 덜덜 떨며 마치 죽었다 깨어난 사람처럼 반쯤 기절한 상태였네. 그는 내 눈 앞에서 다른 사람으로 바뀐 것이네!

그 후 한 시간 동안 그가 나에게 들려준 이야기를 나는 여기에 옮길 수가 없네. 나는 내 눈으로 직접 보았고 그것 때문에 내 영혼은 병이 들었네. 내 인생이 송두리째 흔들렸고 도저히 잠을 이룰 수가 없네. 죽음과 같은 공포가 밤낮으로 내 곁을 떠나지 않네. 살날이 얼마 남지 않은 것 같네. 그리고 나는 내가 본 끔찍한 일을 믿지 못하며 죽겠지.

지킬의 고백에 따르면 그날 밤 우리 집에 온 사람은 하이드라는 자였네. 자네도 지금쯤이면 그가 댄버스 커루 경의 살인범이라는 것을 들었을 테지.

자네의 친구,
헤이스티 래니언

## 7장 | 지킬 박사의 이야기

**p.110~111** 어터슨 씨는 래니언 박사의 편지를 한쪽으로 치워 놓고 믿을 수 없다는 듯이 고개를 저었다. 그리고 헨리 지킬의 사무실에서 발견한 봉투를 열었다. 그는 편지들을 펼쳐서 읽기 시작했다.

나는 상당한 재산이 있는 부유한 집안에서 태어났네. 잘생긴 데다 부지런했고 야심만만했지. 의사가 된 나는 동료와 친구들에게 존경을 받았네. 하지만 내 본성에는 방탕한 면이 있었네. 나는 마약과 술에 중독되었고 육체적인 쾌락에 탐닉했네.

나는 스스로를 억제하려고 애를 썼지만 가끔씩은 그러지를 못했네. 하지만 수년 동안 내 본성의 이러한 측면을 잘 숨겨왔네. 그리고 끔찍한 수치심을 느꼈네.

나는 많은 사람들이 이러한 쾌락을 즐긴다는 것을 알았지만 미래에 대한 나의 높은 기대는 추악한 즐거움을 훨씬 나쁜 것처럼 보이게 했네. 나는 모든 사람이 선과 악 사이에서 끊임없이 투쟁하는 것에 대해 생각하기 시작했고 모든 인간은 그 본성에 실재적이고도 다른 두 가지 면을 가지고 있다는 결론을 내렸네. 그리고 이같은 두 가지 본성이 한 사람 안에서 끊임없이 싸우는 것은 인류의 저주라고 생각했네. 나는 이 두 가지 본성을 분리하는 가능성을 상상하며 실험을 시작했네.

p.112~113 마침내 나는 선택할 때마다 내 본성의 도덕적인 측면은 사라지게 하고 어두운 측면이 나타나게 하리라 믿어지는 약을 발명했다네.

나는 이 약을 사용하기 전에 오래도록 망설였지만 결국 유혹이 너무나 컸네. 어느 늦은 밤, 나는 재료들을 섞었고 그것들이 유리병에서 끓어오르면서 증기가 나는 것을 지켜봤네. 거품이 멈추자, 나는 인생을 바꿔놓을 액체를 마셨네.

곧바로 뼈가 부서지는 듯한 끔찍한 고통과 지독한 메스꺼움을 느꼈네. 내 영혼 깊이 드리워진 공포심은 말로 다 설명할 수가 없네. 그러고 나서 이러한 고통은 사라지기 시작했고 나는 육체적으로 더 젊어지고 이전에는 알 수 없었던 영혼의 자유로움을 경험하면서 건강 상태가 더 좋아진 것을 느꼈네. 나는 곧 이 새로운 인격이 내 본래의 악한 본성보다 열 배는 더 악하다는 것을 알게 되었네. 이 생각을 하자 나는 기뻤네. 나는 양손을 펴서 내가 육체적으로도 변했다는 것을 알게 되었네. 나는 전보다 키가 훨씬 작아졌고 손은 앙상하고 털이 수북했네!

p.114~115 내 사무실에는 거울이 없었지만 나는 변화된 모습을 봐야 했네. 나는 살금살금 걸어 내 방의 거울까지 가서 처음으로 에드워드 하이드를 보았네. 하이드는 헨리 지킬보다 훨씬 작고, 말랐으며 젊다는 것을 알았네. 악은 하이드의 얼굴에 숨김없이 드러났고 기형이라는 인상을 주었지만 나에게는 자연스럽고 인간적으로 보였네. 나는 여전히 내 실험을 완성해야 했네. 나는 나의 선한 면을 영원히 잃어버렸는지 아닌지 아직 알지 못했네. 나는 사무실로 돌아가서, 더 많은 약을 준비해 마셨네. 더 끔찍한 아픔과 고통 뒤에, 나는 헨리 지킬의 인격과 육체 그리고 얼굴을 되찾았네.

다음 날, 나는 소호에 집을 구했고 에드워드 하이드의 이름으로 은행 계좌를 열었네. 하인들에게는 하이드 씨가 가끔 집에 모습을 보일 것이며 그를 정중하게 대하라고 말해두었네.

지킬로서 내가 즐겼던 금지된 쾌락들은 추악하고 위엄이 없는 것이었지만, 에드워드 하이드의 수중에 들어가면 그것들은 극악무도해졌네. 지킬은 에드워드 하이드의 행동에 종종 충격을 받았지만, 그에게는 그를 막을 힘이 없었네.

댄버스 경의 살인이 있기 두 달쯤 전에, 나는 늦은 시각에 집에 돌아왔고 그 다음 날 아침 이상한 느낌이 들어 잠에서 깼네. 아래를 내려다 보니 내 손은 에드워드 하이드의 손이었네!

p.116~117 나는 서둘러 거울로 달려 갔고 두려움으로 온몸의 피가 얼어 붙었네. 헨리 지킬의 모습으로 잠자리에 들었는데 에드워드 하이드로 깨어난 것이었네. 잠시 동안, 나는 공포에 질렸네. 그래서 나는 옷을 입고 사무실로 갔다네. 10분 후에, 지킬 박사의 본래 모습으로 되돌아왔고 아침 식사 자리에 앉아 있었네.

나는 나의 이중생활에 따른 문제점에 대해 좀 더 진지하게 생각하기 시작했네. 나의 일부분인 하이드가 최근 들어 활동이 더욱 빈번해지고 강해지고 있었네. 나의 선한 본성을 붙잡아 두기가 점점 어려워지고 있었네. 이것이 위험할 수 있다는 것을 알고 있었네. 만약 내 본성의 악한 면이 완전히 지배한다면, 에드워드 하이드의 성격으로 영원히 굳어질 것이네,

선한 헨리 지킬은 영원히 사라지게 되는 것이지. 나는 둘 중에서 선택을 해야 한다는 것을 알고 있었고 결국 내 본성의 더 나은 부분을 유지하기로 했네. 하지만 나는 소호의 집을 포기하지도 않았고 하이드의 옷을 없애지도 않았네. 아마 나는 이 선택이 오래 가지 못하리라는 것을 알고 있었네.

하지만 두 달 동안 나는 그 어느 때보다 더 도덕적인 생활을 했네. 얼마 후에, 나는 다시 한 번 욕망으로 고통스러웠네. 하이드는 자유를 얻으려고 몸부림치고 있었네. 마침내, 도덕심이 약해지는 순간을 틈타 나는 약을 조제해서 삼켜 버렸네.

p.118~119 그 전까지 나는 에드워드 하이드의 실제 성격에 대해 진지하게 생각해 본 적이 없었네. 하이드가 도덕 관념이 부족하다는 것은 알았지만 철저하게 악하다는 것은 알지 못했네. 나는 곧 이러한 사실을 알게 되었네. 하이드는 너무 오랫동안 억눌려 있어서 미쳐 으르렁거리며 뛰쳐나왔고 가장 나쁜 짓을 할 준비가 되어 있었네. 무엇이 나로 하여금 댄버스 경을 공격하도록 했는지는 모르겠지만, 나는 가엾고 늙은 그의 몸을 때리고 발로 차고 치면서 희열을 느꼈네. 악에 대한 갈망이 그때만큼은 채워졌다네.

나는 소호에 있는 집으로 달려가서 서류들을 없앴네. 그러고는 실험실로 서둘러 돌아갔네. 하이드는 자신의 범죄에 대해 기뻐했고 약을 만들면서 노래를 흥얼거렸네. 하지만 변화의 고통이 사라지기도 전에, 헨리 지킬은 하느님께 간절히 용서를 구했네. 나는 울면서 기도했고 내 머리 속에서 끔찍한 장면들을 떨쳐내려고 했네. 그리고 그때

나는 문제의 해결책이 생각났네. 하이드가 영원히 사라져야 한다는 것이었지. 나는 하이드가 자주 이용했던 실험동 문을 잠그고, 열쇠를 부러뜨렸네.

그 다음 날 누군가가 살인을 목격했다는 소식이 날아들었네. 하이드의 죄가 세상에 알려진 것이지. 내가 하이드를 잠시 동안만 나오게 한다면, 그는 잡혀서 살인죄로 교수형을 당하고 그러면 나도 죽게 되겠지. 지킬의 인격만이 그를 안전하게 할 수 있었네. 나는 하이드를 영원히 사라지도록 해야 했네.

내가 지난 해 다른 사람들을 돕고 그들의 고통을 덜어주기 위해 얼마나 열심히 일했는지 자네는 알 걸세. 하루하루가 조용하고 대부분 행복하게 지나갔지만 악한 면을 잃어버린 것은 아니었네. 젊은 시절에 그랬던 것처럼 몰래 죄를 짓고 싶은 유혹에 빠지곤 했지만, 다시 하이드를 풀어놓는 것은 꿈도 꾸지 않았네.

p.120~121   어느 날, 나는 햇살을 받으며 리젠트 공원의 벤치에 앉아 있었네. 맑고 청명한 1월의 날이었네. 내 안에 있는 사악한 짐승이 몸부림을 쳤지만 나의 선한 면은 아직 깨어날 준비가 되지 않았네. 나는 내가 지금까지 해 오고 앞으로 할 선행에 대해 생각했네. 그런데 그 때, 끔찍한 역겨움과 전율이 나를 덮쳤네. 그러고 나서 강렬한 흥분과 에너지를 느끼기 시작했네. 나는 옷이 몸에 안 맞아 축 처져 있고, 무릎 위에 놓인 손이 앙상하고 털투성이인 것을 알았네. 다시 한 번 나는 에드워드 하이드가 된 것이었네. 나는 쫓기는 신세에 집도 없는 살인자였네.

내 약들은 사무실의 찬장 안에 있었는데, 어떻게 그것을 손에 넣을 수 있단 말인가? 나는 래니언을 생각해 냈고 어떻게 해야 할지 알았네.

나는 마차를 타고 포틀랜드에 있는 한 호텔로 갔네. 별실을 잡고 각각 래니언과 풀에게 편지 한 통씩을 썼네. 호텔 짐꾼에게 그 편지들을 직접 전해 달라고 부탁했네.

그 후, 나는 하이드로 하루 종일 호텔 방의 난롯가에 앉아 있었네. 어둠이 내리자, 자정까지 얼마나 남았는지 계산하며 래니언의 집으로 갔네.

내가 래니언의 집에서 약을 먹었을 때, 내 오랜 친구의 공포는 나에게 엄청난 영향을 주었네. 나는 더 이상 댄버스 경의 끔찍한 살인 사건에 대한 교수형이 두렵지 않았네. 나를 두렵게 한 것은 하이드가 된다는 공포였네. 나는 집에 와서 잠자리에 들었네.

아침에 깨어났을 때, 기운이 없었지만 기분은 상쾌했고 여전히 나의 모습이었네.

p.122~123 그날 아침 나는 아침 식사 후에 뜰에 나와 있었는데 메스껍고 온몸이 떨렸네. 다시 한 번 하이드가 되기 전에 겨우 사무실에 다다를 수 있었네. 나는 다시 내 모습으로 돌아오기 위해 두 배의 약을 먹었네. 이러한 변화는 점점 더 빈번하게 일어났네. 잠을 자거나 잠시 쉬려고 해도, 하이드로 변했네. 나는 점점 약해졌고 하이드의 힘은 점점 더 강해지는 것 같았네. 하지만 하이드는 내가 자살함으로써 그의 목숨을 끊을 수 있는 내 힘을 두려워했고, 나는 그가 불쌍해지기 시작했네.

내게 필요한 약을 구하기 위해 풀이 런던을 얼마나 뒤지고 다녔는지는 풀에게 들어서 알고 있을 것이네. 아무것도 찾지 못했네. 지금 생각해 보니 처음에 실험에 썼던 가루약에 불순물이 섞여 있었고, 그래서 혼합물이 효과가 있었던 같네.

나는 지금 예전의 약의 마지막 남은 효력을 빌어 이 고백을 마치네. 지금이 헨리 지킬이 사신의 생각을 할 수 있고 거울에 비친 자신의 얼굴을 볼 수 있는 마지막 순간이네. 이 고백을 끝내려면 서둘러야 하네. 이것을 쓰고 있는 동안 변화가 일어난다면, 하이드가 이 편지를 갈기갈기 찢어 버릴 것이네.

내가 펜을 내려 놓고 나의 고백을 봉인하면, 나는 불행한 헨리 지킬의 삶을 끝내는 것이네. 왜냐하면 다음번 변화가 일어나고 하이드가 얼마나 오래 살든, 지금이 내가 진정으로 죽는 순간이기 때문이네.

YBM
Reading
Library
독해력완성프로젝트

YBM
Reading
Library
독해력완성프로젝트

YBM
Reading
Library
독해력완성프로젝트